WALKING THE LINE

Two oldies (and one dodgy hip)
tackle the entire Western Front

Nick and Fiona Jenkins

WETSOCKS BOOKS

Published by WETSOCKS BOOKS,

Hebden Bridge

West Yorkshire.

Map by Graeme Park.

ISBN: 978-1-5272-2581-7

For Ian and Alan,

who would have loved to read this.

Contents

PART ONE

The walk to end all walks   11

Who are we?   13

Our families and the Great War   14

Battlefield tourism and our route   17

Look, no maps…   23

Our inspirations and thanks   27

Music while you read   29

War Child   31

PART TWO

Our route – map   34

Nieuwpoort Bad to Diksmuide   35

Diksmuide to Poelkapelle   40

Poelkapelle to Ieper   43

Ieper to Mesen   48

Mesen to Armentières   52

Armentières to Richebourg   56

Richebourg to Béthune   60

Béthune to Lens   63

Lens to Arras   67

Arras to Auchonvillers   71

Auchonvillers to Albert   73

Albert to Péronne   78

Péronne to Mesnil-St-Nicaise   81

Mesnil-St-Nicaise to Noyon   84

Noyon to Coucy-le-Château   86

Coucy-le-Château to Laon   90

Laon to Chamouille   92

Chamouille to Pontavert   96

Pontavert to Reims   100

Reims   103

Reims to Courmelois   105

Courmelois to Bussy-le-Château   108

Bussy-le-Château to Sainte-Menehould   111

Sainte-Menehould to Varennes-en-Argonne   113

Varennes-en-Argonne to Marre   119

Marre to Verdun   123

Verdun to Saint-Maurice-sous-les-Cotes   128

Saint-Maurice to Heurdicourt-sous-les-Côtes   131

Heurdicourt-sous-les-Côtes to Pont à Mousson   134

Pont à Mousson to Alaincourt-la-Côte   137

Alaincourt-la-Côte to Château Salins   140

Château Salins to Tarquimpol   142

Tarquimpol to Blamont   145

Blamont to Pierre Percée   149

Pierre Percée to Saint-Dié-des-Vosges   153

Saint-Dié-des-Vosges to Sainte-Marie-aux-Mines   156

Sainte-Marie-aux-Mines to Fréland   159

Fréland to Munster   162

Munster to Guebwiller   167

Guebwiller to Cernay   169

Cernay to Carspach   172

Carspach to Mooslargue   175

Mooslargue to Kilometre Zero   178

What have we learnt?   183

Postscript   187

More to Read   188

PART ONE

The walk to end all walks

It was an ambitious plan: to walk the entire First World War Western Front, from Nieuwpoort on the Channel coast in Belgium to the Swiss border near Pfetterhouse and Mooslargue, in the centenary year of the 1918 armistice. It sounds simple, but it is a long, long way. The Front is reckoned to be 440 miles long as the crow flies - though, of course, our walk was likely to be very much longer as we aren't crows and we couldn't just follow the original trench system.

Could we do it in one go? We genuinely had no idea. Our intention was to walk away from the Belgian beaches and see how far we could get. We had to be practical: we would need food and accommodation along the way, so our route would have to bear that in mind. We didn't expect that to be a problem at the beginning, but we were likely to be passing through more remote areas later, where bed and board could become more of an issue. Not every French town or village has a café, hotel or even boulangerie these days.

It would be nice to say we were following the exact route of the First World War No Man's Land, though if we were going to attempt to walk such a long way, we couldn't afford to get bogged down in ploughed fields or impenetrable woods. Inevitably there would be TGV railway lines, autoroutes, industrial estates and military zones that we would have to (or want to) avoid.

We might therefore need to veer away from the front line so we didn't end up sleeping under a tree or trying to run across a six-lane motorway. In any case, although the Western Front was largely static, there was some movement over the years between 1914 and 1918, so it is impossible to plot an exact line.

How long would it take? We had no idea. We were allowing up to three months, though we were only too aware that anything could happen to stop us in our tracks: illness or accidents along the way, unexpected crises at home… we were keeping an open mind and simply intended to keep putting one foot in front of the other for as long as we could. The important thing was to get started.

As Chinese philosopher Lao Tzu said more than 2,500 years ago: "The journey of a thousand miles begins with a single step." Fiona's Fitbit would be keeping track of exactly how many steps followed that initial one.

Three important things to bear in mind:

1. We are not "war buffs". We have been interested in the First World War for many years (at one time, our daughters believed no holiday was complete without a visit to a war cemetery) but we are not obsessed with the minutiae of battles or strategy.

2. This was not a sightseeing trip: we have already been to some of the key locations on the Western Front and no doubt we would find interesting places along the way. However we would never get anywhere if we kept stopping.

3. This was certainly not a "celebration" of the war. The First World War was horrendous, casting a sinister shadow over the century that followed. People from all over the world were drawn into the conflict and civilian and military casualties are estimated at around 37 million. Almost seven million civilians and 10 million military personnel died. We aimed to honour their memory but not glorify the war in which they were forced to take part. There was little glory - but there was a lot of sacrifice.

Who are we?

We are a (fairly) normal early-retired couple, well into our 60s (though not yet receiving our state pensions, which seem to be receding into the distance faster than we can walk) and only moderately fit. We do like walking, though, and we try to make sure Fiona hits at least 10,000 steps on her Fitbit every day.

We both gave up the day jobs in 2015. Fiona was a librarian and Nick a journalist, but she is also a musician with 35 years' experience as a piano teacher and he is a cognitive hypnotherapist and former aromatherapist.

We live in Hebden Bridge in West Yorkshire and in the Dordogne in France - both of which are good walking areas. Hebden Bridge is in the upper Calder Valley in the Pennines and it's brilliant for the leg muscles: everything is either up or down.

Fiona has been fighting a painful hip for some time and is waiting for a replacement, though she often finds it easier to walk than to sit down (and her doctor says she must keep exercising), so we were hoping this adventure wouldn't be too difficult.

We had put our legs to the test before making any irreversible plans. Last year we managed to walk the full length of the Rochdale Canal in two days without serious problems. That was 26 miles from our front door in Hebden Bridge to Manchester one day, and an easier six miles in the other direction to Sowerby Bridge the next. We reckoned that if we could do that, we could cope with moderate distances every day.

The timing of the walk was slightly problematic for Nick, as it happened at the end of a football season in which his team Fulham were playing for promotion. Would they go up to the Premier League automatically – or would they qualify for a Wembley play-off final, so that he would miss his first opportunity to see his team play there since 1975?

Our families and the Great War

Many people have asked us if any of our family members died in the First World War.

All of our grandfathers served in the British armed forces – and fortunately, all four survived. Fiona's grandmother Effie also played a vital role during the war as a nurse.

Jack and Effie Day

(Fiona's paternal grandparents)

John Thomas Day was born in Hetton-le-Hole in the coalfields of Co Durham in 1896. At the age of 14 he was a blacksmith's assistant at the Hetton Lyons mine, but he later worked his way up to a clerk's job in the colliery office.

Jack signed up on October 27 1915, at the age of 19. He served in the Royal Artillery in France and was given the rank of bombardier in 1918. He used to tell fascinating stories of life at the Front, including the hazards of being an artillery spotter while suspended under a hot air balloon. Jack was discharged in 1918 "as miner", without any disability, though he had been admitted to hospital in France suffering from concussion - an injury he picked up playing football.

Effie Richardson Wight was a bakery assistant in Edinburgh when war broke out, and she decided she wanted to be a nurse. In 1917 she was old enough to start work at the Edinburgh War Hospital: "I went straight on to the wards - and I wanted to run back home," she told The Scotsman in 1988, as she described the horrors she witnessed.

Effie's experiences in that hospital made her a lifelong pacifist.

John William Lacey

(Fiona's maternal grandfather)

John, also known as Jack, was a 21-year-old clerk when he enlisted in Newcastle upon Tyne in November 1914. He served with the West Yorkshire Regiment - and was wounded in France in 1916 - until he was commissioned as an officer in the Northumberland Fusiliers in 1917. He was discharged in March 1919.

His war records highlight the fact that he spoke German, a language he had learnt in his pre-war civilian job.

Henry Wilson Baker

(Nick's maternal grandfather)

Henry (known as Hal) was born in London in 1890 and was a married librarian when he signed up as a full-time soldier in March 1915. He was shipped immediately to France, where he spent most of the war, finally being discharged in March 1919.

Some years ago, we had his medals framed and the shop owner said: "You know he was in the Army Service Corps so probably didn't see any action?" He said it as though we should be disappointed.

We weren't.

Leslie Roberts Jenkins

(Nick's paternal grandfather)

Leslie was born in Henley-on-Thames in 1900, so was only 14 when the war began.

He joined up in June 1918, just before his 18th birthday, and it seems from his records that he wanted to be a pilot but was passed fit to be an observer.

Nick recalls his grandfather telling him that this involved standing in the rear cockpit of the biplane while keeping watch. Luckily for him, the war ended before he saw active service in what sounds like a very dangerous occupation. His records reveal that he was awarded an honorary commission in 1919 after being demobilised.

Battlefield tourism and our route

The first battlefield tourists started arriving on the Western Front not long after the 1918 Armistice, as families travelled to see where their loved ones had fought and, in many cases, died. They were encouraged by Michelin guides to the battlefield areas. But by the later decades of the 20th century, visitor numbers were dwindling.

In the last 20 years or so, there has been a huge surge in interest in the First World War - no doubt partly driven by school curricula and educational visits, but also by a renewed fascination in family history.

When we and our friends were children, our grandfathers didn't speak much of what they saw in the war. Now, of course, there is nobody left with first-hand experience. If we want to get close to the experience of that generation, we have to travel to Belgium and France ourselves.

We first travelled to the Somme in the early 1990s when our daughters were young. We camped in Péronne and toured with a copy of Martin and Mary Middlebrook's brilliant book The Somme Battlefields. Martin Middlebrook - whom Nick met at the Thiepval commemoration of the 80th anniversary of the Battle of the Somme on July 1 1996 – also wrote the definitive work The First Day On The Somme in 1971.

The Somme Battlefields was first published in 1991, just as interest in the Western Front was being rekindled, and it remains an indispensable guide.

His "Helpful Information" chapter, for example, describes the process that led to the creation of the cemeteries that are scattered across all First World War battlefields, and which make for such poignant visits. On our walk we would no doubt be calling in at many of these graveyards, which are all beautifully maintained to this day.

Many visitors come to seek out the last resting place of a relative, but others simply wonder at the scale of the killing while enjoying the peace where once there was deadly chaos. Some War Graves Commission cemeteries are enormous, such as Tyne Cot near Ieper (Ypres), in Belgium, containing the graves of soldiers whose bodies were collected from across a wide area.

Others are small, with a cemetery created around the men's original burial place. One such is the Devonshire Cemetery near Mametz on the Somme, where more than 160 men of one regiment were buried in a row in their own trench. A wooden sign was erected bearing an inscription that is now engraved in stone: "The Devonshires held this trench; the Devonshires hold it still."

Inevitably, modern life and the need to build homes, factories and main roads has put pressure on the preserved battlefields, but the French and Belgians have generally been good at honouring those who fought on their soil.

And, of course, the process of unearthing the dead continues. Bodies are still being exhumed and reburied in war cemeteries. Sometimes they are identified and family are invited to the burial ceremony, but often they are the unknown bodies of men whose names are listed as the Missing on memorials such as Thiepval and Tyne Cot.

In the last 20 years there has been a growth in battlefield archaeology. After the Armistice, there was an understandable rush to return to normal, so trenches were quickly filled in as farmers worked to reclaim their land. Some trenches are now being reopened by archaeologists, who are discovering buried evidence of what happened there 100 years ago.

Meanwhile, farmers are still ploughing up live ammunition and explosives in what has long been known as the Iron Harvest. Battlefield visitors will still find rusty shells piled up at the side of the road, awaiting collection and disposal.

These should, of course, never be touched as they are volatile and potentially very dangerous.

We would NOT be collecting souvenirs on our walk, though there are many who do. Many years ago we visited the museum below the basilica in Albert on the Somme. In those days they were selling items salvaged from the battlefields.

Our daughter wanted something and we weren't keen on buying her the rusty bullets or twisted rifle barrels, so we chose a bag of a British officer's tunic buttons. Perfectly safe - though it was only later that we started to think about the last person to use those buttons.

Over the years, we revisited those areas - Nick worked then at the Yorkshire Post and often wrote battlefield tourism articles when the paper produced supplements marking First World War anniversaries.

In 1996 we visited Ieper and stood with a modest crowd to hear the bugler play the Last Post under the Menin Gate - a ceremony that has taken place at 8pm every night since 1929, other than during the German occupation from 1940 to 1944. Now that ceremony always attracts huge crowds. Many of those pilgrims visit the battlefields with specialist tour groups, while others make their own way there.

We are definitely in the latter group.

The Western Front extended from the Belgian coast to the Swiss border. In general terms, therefore, it starts flat, becomes hillier and ends up crossing the Vosges mountains. So we were starting with the easier bit. Belgium and northern France are flat and well-populated, so walking should be easy and finding hotels, B&Bs, restaurants and shops shouldn't be too much of an issue - but we would have to see how things developed after that.

From the coast at Nieuwpoort Bad, we aimed to pass through Flanders and Picardy, then on through the Somme, the Aisne, the Chemin des Dames, Champagne, the Argonne, Verdun, and the Vosges.

When we think of the warfare of the Western Front, we have an image of the classic trench: dug in deep, with firesteps at the front, ladders to climb over the parapet, and dug-outs at the back. Trenches were usually cut in a zigzag pattern to protect soldiers from explosions and make it easier to resist an invasion by enemy troops. Behind the front line were communication trenches that allowed troops to move up from the rear. Of course, much of the Western Front trench system was built like this, but there were exceptions.

To begin at the beginning, the race to the sea that created the static war of the trenches ended up, not surprisingly, at the sea. So trenches were dug in the sand of the Channel beaches on each side of the estuary at Nieuwpoort Bad.

Bizarrely, as Peter Barton recounts in The Battlefields Of The First World War, night-time patrols were sent out from these trenches - but instead of walking out into No Man's Land, they swam into the sea, equipped with revolvers strapped to the top of their heads.

Further along the line, the water table was high enough to make deep trenches a problem. We are familiar now with the condition of trench foot, caused by standing for too long in the water that gathered at the bottom of the trenches. This foul water caused all sorts of problems but could not be drained away. Sometimes men had to stand for lengthy periods in water that came up to their waists. Elsewhere, it was impossible to dig deep at all, due to the rocky ground. Instead, trenches were created by building upwards - throwing up solid barricades of sandbags, soil, rock or concrete - rather than digging deep into the earth.

As the opposing sides dug in following the more traditional open battles that began the war, each raced to grab the most commanding positions. The slightest elevation made observation and defence easier, so both sides wanted the higher ground.

One of the most fought-over elevations of the Ypres battlefield was Hill 60. It was a spoil heap created by railway builders and only 60 feet above sea level, but it afforded such a good view that it was the scene of fierce fighting and mine-blowing - so much so that today it is only 13 feet high.

On average, the opposing front lines were about 250 yards apart, but the width of No Man's Land between the trenches varied enormously. At some places in the Vosges, where the terrain is particularly rocky and inhospitable, enemy troops were barely 30 yards apart – sometimes closer.

One hundred years on, much of the evidence of this digging has become hidden by the agriculture that resumed after the war, the growth of trees and vegetation (the area around Verdun was deliberately forested as it was believed it could never fully recover), or by the natural erosion of time.

But plenty of evidence remains, and archaeologists are opening up filled-in trenches and tunnels all the time. At Vimy Ridge we once visited the trench system preserved by the Canadians, and at Beaumont-Hamel we have explored Newfoundland Park, where the trenches remain but their edges have been allowed to soften and grass over naturally. The park is a rare survival - a place where you can walk from one clearly-defined frontline trench, across No Man's Land, and into the enemy trenches. No soldier managed that on July 1 1916.

Elsewhere, obvious signs have disappeared but, especially in winter when the fields have been ploughed, the outlines of the trenches can sometimes be seen from the sky. The war ended in 1918 and normal life gradually resumed for the displaced residents of the battlefield areas, but the landscape is still scarred and will no doubt remain so for many decades to come.

We have been thinking about doing this walk for a long time (we remember telling Nick's dad about our plans, and he died in 2007) but we are not the only ones to have had the idea. Historian Sir Anthony Seldon is a leading figure behind a project to create a permanent long-distance footpath along the entire length of the Front.

His inspiration was a letter home from the Front, written in 1915 by Alexander Douglas Gillespie, a young officer in the Argyll and Sutherland Highlanders. He wrote: "When peace comes, our government might combine with the French government to make one long avenue between the lines from the Vosges to the sea... I would make a fine broad road in the No Man's Land between the lines, with paths for pilgrims on foot and plant trees for shade and fruit trees, so the soil should not altogether be waste... we might make the most beautiful road in all the world."

Another founding trustee of the Western Front Way is BBC Countryfile presenter Tom Heap, who, as one of Gillespie's great-nephews, inherited many of his letters home. He said: "I feel it is an idea whose time has come. It's important for people to continue to remember and visit the Western Front. It also isn't necessarily morbid. It should be a place where people can laugh."

Look, no maps

The wonders of modern technology: we were not carrying any paper maps with us on our walk. Instead we took a Samsung Galaxy S2, an eight-inch tablet that, of course, has access to Google Maps when it is online. More importantly, it was loaded with Memory Map and was GPS-enabled.

This meant that we would be following the IGN 1:25,000 maps – the French equivalent of the Ordnance Survey walkers' maps - on the tablet. So no need for a huge pile of paper maps.

Even more exciting: Linesman was loaded on to the tablet. This is a collection of hundreds of contemporary First World War trench maps that have been geo-referenced and can therefore be overlaid on modern maps.

What this meant is that as we walked along, we could plot a route on the modern map, then flip between old trench maps – all the while following our exact location thanks to GPS.

We would be crossing and re-crossing old front lines many times during our walk. Nowadays there is often very little obvious evidence of wartime activity after 100 years but at least we would know where to look.

We just had to make sure we didn't spend the entire walk staring at the tablet (Fiona reckons Nick spends way too much time staring at a screen anyway). The GPS meant, in theory at least, that we should never get lost. So we were not carrying maps…what WERE we carrying?

We were inspired to do this walk by many people, but we were particularly grateful for the advice gleaned from the website of two Australians, Jenny and Keith, who spend their summers walking in France and (it seems) their winters writing about it and planning the next one. They have a golden rule, which makes perfect sense when you have to carry all your stuff on your back all day: apart from rainwear and something warm, don't carry anything you won't use/wear every day.

We wanted to travel as light as possible, so took their advice. A friend, Peter Beal, who once walked from Land's End to John O'Groats, reminded us that by the time he reached Bristol on his epic walk, he put much of his gear in a parcel and posted it home. We didn't want to be troubling the French postal service.

Our original plan was, like Jenny and Keith, to carry simple camping gear. They camp when they can, and it's true that being able to camp would have given us greater freedom and flexibility. But we decided to prioritise comfort (especially given Fiona's bad hip) so we left the tent at home.

Fiona would be missing her piano while we were away, but we decided not to carry it with us - or to pack her accordion in our rucksacks.

Our luggage included two "luxuries" that would be returning to France for the first time in a century.

The first is a silver cigarette case belonging to Fiona's grandfather. It is engraved "J. Wm. Lacey, Blyth" and its hallmark tells us it came from Birmingham in 1915. It is almost certainly a gift to Jack, probably from his mother. On the back there is a large dent - though we can only guess at whether that happened during Jack's time at the front line.

The second is a battered New Testament "Presented to Pte H. W. Baker by friends in St Albans, with good wishes, in commemoration of the stay of the troops in the City. 1915." On the opposite page is a copy of a handwritten message from Lord Roberts, telling soldiers that "you will find in this little book guidance when you are in health, comfort when you are in sickness, and strength when you are in adversity".

Lord Roberts was the last commander-in-chief of British forces (the post was abolished in 1904) and died aged 82 while visiting Indian troops in France in November 1914. Nick's paternal grandfather and father were given their middle name Roberts in tribute to him. We wouldn't be smoking or reading the New Testament on the trip, but we carried both these objects with us as links to the grandfathers who served in France and Belgium in the First World War.

Apart from that, our basic luggage list was as follows:

One rucksack each (Nick's is an Osprey Kestrel 68, and Fiona's a Mountain Warehouse Peru 55L) - which turned out to be too big for what we were actually carrying as we bought them with camping in mind.

Clothes:

Walking shoes: Nick's were Meindl Respond GTX and Fiona's were North Face Ultra Fastpack III GTX (what IS it with GTX...?!) - both pairs chosen for comfort

Two T-shirts each
Long-sleeved T-shirt each
Walking trousers with detachable legs
Pair shorts (Nick)
Skirt (Fiona)
Flat pumps
Underwear and socks - spares of each
Uniqlo down jackets that weigh virtually nothing but are very warm
Folding rain jackets and trousers (nothing more dispiriting than getting wet through with little prospect of getting dry)
Sun hats
Sunglasses
Pair of trekking poles each

One Swiss Army-style knife - including corkscrew, of course.

First aid:

Sun screen
Painkillers
Plasters/Compeed

Vaseline and clotrimazole cream (you don't want to know why)
Antihistamines

Toiletries:

Toothbrushes and paste
Deodorant
Moisturiser
Mini hairbrush
Contact lenses/case/fluid for Nick
Travel shaver

Mobile phones
Samsung Galaxy 8-inch tablet, loaded with Linesman trench
map system and IGN maps
Lightweight keyboard for blogging
Universal charger/power pack
Fiona's Fitbit, which would measure our distances each day
Fiona's reading glasses
Notebook and pen
Kindle
Passports
Small purse

Emergency rations:

Chocolate for when blood sugar levels threaten to run low (rarely
a good thing…)
Insulated pouches so chocolate doesn't melt

Given that we would be wearing much of the above, we hoped this
would not mean too much to carry.

And if we needed anything else, France does have shops.

Our inspirations – and thanks

We have been idly planning this walk for many years, but several people have encouraged us to put that planning into action.

The first is Stephen O'Shea, who walked the Western Front 25 to 30 years ago, when the battlefield areas were less well visited. See the bibliography at the end for details of his very readable book, to which we are indebted for the basic route of our walk. He kindly shared some thoughts with us about our journey.

A few years ago, Fiona discovered Jenny and Keith, "a pair of ageing but energetic Australians, addicted to walking in France", and their excellent website – walkinginfrance.info - in which they recount their adventures. They haven't walked in the battlefield areas, but we have read their "Beginner's guide" to walking in France and their "Golden rules" VERY carefully.

In a quiet moment at work (and there weren't many of them), Nick found the story of Mike and Janet Higgins, a couple in their 60s who walked from their home in Shropshire to their apartment on Lake Garda in Italy. Unless we take a horrible wrong turning, their 1,424-mile walk makes ours look like a gentle stroll, but we are grateful to them for proving this can be done.

Nick's former colleague Peter Beal, a man who regarded a marathon as a Sunday afternoon training run, celebrated his retirement by walking from Land's End to John O'Groats and he continues to go long-distance walking with his wife. He has very kindly shared his hard-won experience with us.

Then there is Dave Cornthwaite, a man we first came across at a Lost Lectures event at a famous boxing venue, the York Hall in Bethnal Green, east London. He was on the bill alongside Ruby Wax and psychologist Simon Baron Cohen – all delivering talks from the ring. We were so impressed by Dave – a self-confessed couch potato who reinvented himself and set out on a number of

1,000-mile challenges – that Nick suggested him as a speaker at a Quest Institute event for cognitive hypnotherapists, where he went down a storm.

We like his slogan: Say Yes More. But not all the time, as Dave himself says, because that would be stupid.

Special thanks to Jerry Whitehead at Great War Digital, who went to a lot of trouble to load our tablet with Memory Map and Linesman. We are massively grateful.

We are also grateful to firstworldwar.com for providing the information for the On This Day feature at the top of each day's entry.

Huge thanks too to graphics wizard Graeme Park for the excellent mapping.

Music while you read

Fiona has put some music videos on YouTube featuring recordings of her playing.

The first is an instrumental version of Eric Bogle's great anti-war song variously known as No Man's Land or Green Fields Of France. Many singers have recorded this 1976 song - as well as his other war classic And The Band Played Waltzing Matilda - but we reckon no one has ever bettered June Tabor's 1977 version, which never fails to bring a tear to the eye.

Fiona recorded hers on a Yamaha Clavinova piano.

The other tune, The Battle Of The Somme, was written during the war by William Laurie, pipe major of the 8th Argylls, who fought in that battle and died shortly afterwards.

Bagpipers led Scottish regiments into battle, making it a very dangerous profession, but they also played laments - such as Flowers Of The Forest at military funerals - and retreats, which is what this tune is. Not necessarily to be played while retreating from the enemy, but for playing, for example, at the end of the day.

It's a stirring tune that featured in the memorable 1978 National Theatre promenade production of Lark Rise To Candleford (not to be confused with the recent TV soap of that name). It was played by the Albion Band after the vicar read the names from the (real) village church's war memorial. One of Nick's all-time great emotional theatrical moments.

As Fiona doesn't play the bagpipes, this tune was played on the accordion.

Incidentally, the picture on the Battle Of The Somme video was taken by Nick on July 1 1996, after a ceremony at Thiepval to commemorate the 80th anniversary of the first day of the battle. After meeting some of the veterans, well into their 100s, he walked down the sunken road towards the Ulster Tower - and met some WW1 re-enactors coming the other way. It was a moment to make the hairs stand up on the back of your head.

Chanson De Craonne is a song we heard about when visiting the ruins of Craonne on the Chemin des Dames. It was a soldiers' anti-war song that was linked with military mutinies and was banned in France until 1974. Fiona has given it a suitable honkytonk treatment.

Adieu Les Filles De Mon Pays (Goodbye To The Girls Of My Country) is a song, dating from the First World War, that was traditionally played as French soldiers marched away to war.

The videos can be found on YouTube on the 2018 Walk The Line channel (just search for Fiona Jenkins walktheline).

War Child

It was supposed to be "the war that ends all wars" - but when the next one began, the Great War had to be renamed.

In No Man's Land, Eric Bogle's tragic song about the futility of conflict, the songwriter imagines sitting at the graveside of a Great War soldier named Willie McBride:

"And I can't help but wonder now, Willie McBride,
Do all those who lie here know why they died?
Did you really believe them when they told you the cause?
Did you really believe that this war would end wars?
But the suffering, the sorrow, the glory, the shame,
The killing, the dying, it was all done in vain,
For Willie McBride it's all happened again,
And again, and again, and again, and again."

Sadly, war does happen again and again and again. And, of course, it's not just the troops who suffer. The scale of the First World War meant that millions of civilians were killed or displaced, including children - the most innocent victims of all.

And children continue to suffer from the effects of wars they neither understand nor want. That is why we decided to support UK-based charity War Child on our walk. Although it was not strictly a charity walk - and we were entirely self-funded - we decided it would be a shame to miss the opportunity to do some good with our adventure.

War Child says: "We aim to reach children as early as possible when conflict breaks out, and stay on to support them - long after the TV cameras have gone home. We help keep them safe, give them an education, and equip them with skills for the future.

"We understand children's needs, respect their rights, and put them at the centre of everything we do. Whether it's helping Syrian children access education, rehabilitating ex-child soldiers in the Central African Republic or seeking justice for young people detained in Afghanistan.

"We also work with children and young people to change systems and practices that affect them. We campaign on the root causes of conflict, and we demand that children are at the centre of all humanitarian responses."

To find out more about the work of War Child, and maybe make a donation, take a look at its website – warchild.org.uk.

PART TWO

Over the top and on our way

On this day 1915: Zeppelin raid on East Anglia, plane bombs Faversham and Sittingbourne in Kent.

Day One: Nieuwpoort Bad to Diksmuide
Miles today: 16

The First World War didn't happen overnight - but it wasn't as long in the planning as this walk. We've been talking about it for a dozen years, so we were probably as surprised as anyone to find ourselves actually starting out from Nieuwpoort Bad, the seaside resort where the Western Front met the English Channel.

We'd set off from our front door in Hebden Bridge yesterday, walking to the station. When we arrived at Hull Paragon station, via Leeds, we decided this was a walking trip, so no cabs. Three and a half miles to the docks took us past the massive wind turbine blades lined up outside the Siemens factory. Then through the deserted passenger terminal and on to a nearly-empty ship. This morning, the only people actually walking out of the port were us – heading for the wonderful Kusttram (coastal tram), which took us to Nieuwpoort Bad, our jumping-off point. A bargain three euros for a one hour and 40 minute ride.

Time for a selfie by the mouth of the Yser river – we'd planned to ask a passer-by to take a picture of us but there wasn't one - and we were off. We began on a boardwalk heading past the glitzy marina and new homes of the resort, walking back towards Nieuwpoort town, where we were looking for the path to Diksmuide.

We found it first time and were just congratulating ourselves when we spotted the yellow and black tape ahead. The bridge over the Diksmuide-Dunkerque canal is being rebuilt so there was no way across. This was when we became truly aware of the Belgian love of bikes. A cycle detour was clearly marked, but it didn't look any good for walkers. And that was something we noticed throughout the day. At the mouth of the Yser we'd noticed a sign about GRs (grande randonnée long-distance walking paths) – and there was one to our destination of Diksmuide! It was number 131 and it was marked blue.

Well, we reckon we walked that path, but we never once saw a GR sign, let alone a blue one. We rapidly came to the conclusion that Belgium loves cyclists but it's not so keen on walkers. Or maybe it just doesn't love the French and their fancy GRs... Anyway, a detour down the canal to the Pelican bridge and back to where we failed to find an open bridge before, and we were off again.

Oddly – and maybe we'd been confused by the detour – it took us a while to realise we were walking on the trackbed of the old Nieuwpoort to Diksmuide railway. A railway of huge significance during the First World War because of the local geography. In the autumn of 1914, the Germans were threatening to overrun the Allies in this sector. Then someone had the brilliant idea of flooding the fields. Given that those fields were actually below sea level at high tide (protected only by a system of dykes, drainage channels and canals), it was remarkably easy to recreate an inland sea and hold the German tide at bay. And that is why the apparently insignificant railway embankment was so significant: it was raised above that inland sea.

So it didn't take long before we started noticing wartime relics: the first blockhouse, the concrete observation post at what was once Ramskapelle station...Fiona even claimed to see a Great War ambulance on the motorway we walked under, though Nick, inevitably, was looking in the wrong direction at the time. And, of course, the first war cemetery of our walk – the Belgian one at Ramskapelle.

The path was easy walking – flat, straight and no need for any navigation – but it was long. After a while the Yser Tower, a monument to peace and to Flemish nationalism, appeared on the horizon. It's in Diksmuide, our destination, and it was a long way away. It didn't seem to get much closer. Although the landscape was pretty featureless apart from the occasional farm, there was the occasional sight. The remains of a medieval moated farm on our left, and some odd brick structures on our right, built into the embankment.

We were discussing whether they were war or railway-related when a reconstruction appeared just ahead of us. Because it was so difficult to dig into the wet soil, it turns out the Allies built brick shelters against the side of the railway embankment, roofed them, and covered them with sandbags. And the reconstruction, from 2008, demonstrated just that. Behind the reconstructed shelter was a short length of narrow-gauge railway, to show how supplies were brought up to the front.

We didn't start walking until 12.15 so the afternoon was wearing on as the Yser Tower gradually grew closer.

Along the route were occasional information boards and, reading one of them, Fiona let out a shout. We were in Pervijze – once known as Pervyse, the place where two daring young British women set up a first aid station right behind the front line. We had discovered Elsie Knocker and Mairi Chisholm – dubbed the Madonnas of Pervyse - in a photographic exhibition in Bradford a few months earlier and had brought a book about them to read along the way. On our first day we had accidentally arrived in the village that made them famous.

We kept plodding on and were on the verge of walking – pretty slowly by then – into the outskirts of Diksmuide, looking forward to our hotel, when a friendly older couple stopped us and asked where we were from.

They then insisted on us walking with them – retracing our steps some of the way – on what they said was a "nicer" way into Diksmuide. This probably added a mile or two to our walk, but they were right. And they were lovely – ex-teachers, aged 82 and 75 ("he's got a bad leg," she said, but he raced on ahead).

Anyway, she told us that our way into town was blocked because more First World War bodies were being excavated. She took us to the edge of the Grote Markt, where our hotel is, helpfully pointing out Lidl on the way.

So it added a bit to our walk, but we saw things we would otherwise have missed, including the first British war graves of the walk, at the back of a civilian cemetery – and it was interesting to talk to her (he didn't speak any English).

Just as it was interesting to talk to the old soldiers we met on the ferry, who were off on a battlefield tour. Not of the First World War battlefields, but of the Second – a timely reminder that this land has been fought over more than once.

They were all ex-Royal Hussars and they talked about the Hussars and the Dragoons. We said that sounded like something from Napoleonic times and they told us they still wear that gear as mess uniform, including spurs (even though they drive tanks these days). They said their tour guide had some surprises for them. "Maybe it'll include a knocking shop," said one hopefully. "Though these days we'd all deserve a medal if we could manage it..."

Diksmuide was right in the thick of it during the First World War and my old maps show trenches right through the town. But, like so many war-damaged European towns, it rebuilt itself in the

1920s and today the Grote Markt (market square) is as pretty as it ever was.

As for us, today's walk was longer than expected, but we survived. An unexpected hotel bath, steak and chips and a couple of beers across the square later, we are ready for tomorrow, which SHOULD be shorter. The next couple of days' walking, we hope, are the easier strolls we should have given ourselves today. But at least we have proved we can do it.

We've started!

A beacon for peace

On this day 1918: North-west of Diksmuide, Belgians take 700 prisoners and 42 machine guns.

Day Two: Diksmuide to Poelkapelle
Today's miles: 13
Total miles: 29

We debated over breakfast whether we should start the day with a visit to the Yser Tower, the huge concrete structure that served as a beacon yesterday. We decided we should - and we're glad that we did.

The tower was built after the Second World War to replace a smaller post-WW1 tower that was dynamited in 1946 in protest at the Flemish nationalists who helped the Nazis. The rubble from

the original tower was used to build a peace arch as an entrance to the new tower's garden. Rusty old shell cases and other battlefield bricabrac have since been used to fashion sculptures around the grounds.

When Stephen O'Shea visited the tower for his 1996 book Back To The Front, he found it full of dusty exhibits and a rallying point for crusty old Flemish nationalists. It seems that in the latter decades of the 20th century it had become a magnet for unpleasant nationalists from all over Europe. Not any more.

It is now an out and out peace monument (the tallest in Europe, it boasts) and these days the nationalists have been replaced by hundreds of schoolchildren bussed in to learn about the horrors of war.

The primary school children were spared the short introductory film - a gruelling few minutes reconstructing life in the trenches - but this gave us the most realistic idea of front line life and death we had ever seen.

In the lift to the 22nd floor, and up the stairs to the open deck - and what a view. We could see the route we took yesterday, and also that our walking friend had been right: there WAS an excavation for bodies that has resulted in the old railway line path being blocked off. These excavations continue all over northern France and Belgium and any bodies found are given a proper burial in war cemeteries with full honours.

If they can be identified, as they often can, the dead man's name is removed from the monument to the missing on which his death was previously recorded.

The tower's museum, far from being dusty, was as up to date as any we have visited, explaining in graphic form the struggles of the Belgian people as their country was invaded. We could have spent a lot longer there. It is very much a peace museum, with the words No More War in four languages. The children were entranced. Though that didn't stop the boys being typical boys and pretending to fire guns at each other as they left the tower. We set off from there on today's walk, initially following the main road to

Ypres. Our online map told us we were walking right along a frontline trench. Our eyes told me this was a pretty busy road these days.

One good thing about Belgium's obsession with cycling, though, is that there is always a bike path at the side of the main carriageway. As long as we walked facing the traffic, so we could see any cyclists coming our way, we were safe.

It was, nevertheless, a relief to turn off to the left, along some peaceful and largely traffic-free suburban village roads.

Today's walk across the Flanders plains was unsurprisingly pretty flat, though we did at least rise above sea level. This afternoon, we walked up a gentle slope to a spot called 19 Metre Hill on my British trench map. So, not that much of a hill really.

Naming on those maps was interesting. Presumably the British gave their own names to buildings and geographical features. One can only assume it was a metallurgist who named everything Tin, Tungsten, Lead etc. We preferred whoever it was who went for musical names: Brahms, Beethoven and Mozart Farms, Paganini Crossroads - and Lakmé corner, where we ate our sandwiches.

Tonight's lodging is a hotel in the converted old town hall of Poelkapelle, run by a young couple who cooked us an excellent dinner. It seems appropriate to drink beer here, rather than wine, and our host ran us through the lengthy list, pointing out that most are probably a good deal stronger than we are used to.

And a lot tastier than many continental beers, but we were mindful of that warning over the alcoholic strength as we need to sleep well to prepare ourselves for tomorrow. The next place on our itinerary is Ieper (Ypres), a place that looms large in the history of the 20th century.

Wiping away a tear in Wipers

On this day 1916: Deportation of civilians announced in Lille and elsewhere in northern France.

Day Three: Poelkapelle to Ieper (Ypres)
Miles today: 11.5
Total miles: 40.5

It's impossible not be moved when the first bugle notes are played at the nightly Last Post Ceremony under the Menin Gate in the town once known as Ypres.

The gateway was built as a monument to 54,000 men from Britain and its colonies whose bodies were never found, each name carved into the stone panels that reach up to the roof, at the point where most of them marched out of the town to their deaths.

Every night since 1929 - apart from a four-year break during the Nazi occupation - the buglers of the Ieper (Ypres) fire brigade have played the Last Post. Crowds start to gather well before the 8pm start and, even on a Wednesday night in April, there were many people laying wreaths as part of the nightly ceremony.

But it hasn't always been like this. By the 1950s and 60s there was little interest in attending. It's said that the buglers - up to four of them - sometimes outnumbered the spectators.

Renewed interest in the First World War, though, means spectators now have to arrive early, or stretch, to get a view.

Tonight the four buglers were joined by a piper from the Royal Scottish Regiment, who played Flowers Of The Forest. One of the

regiment's officers read the Lawrence Binyon Exhortation ("They shall not grow old...") and two NCOs laid wreaths.

So far so military. But the kilted soldiers were followed by young people, in twos and threes, stepping forward to lay wreaths in memory of men who must have been their great-grandfathers at the very least.

Of course, we couldn't have missed this ceremony, which we last witnessed in 1996. Even if it meant a shorter walking day today to make sure we spent a night in Ieper.

It's one of the few things we have planned as we generally prefer serendipity to deciding in advance exactly what we want to do and see. So it was that we allowed Stijn, our host last night in Poelkapelle, to suggest a route to Ieper that avoided main roads.

At breakfast this morning he presented us with a printout from a Belgian website for cyclists (OBVIOUSLY not for walkers...what kind of a weirdo goes walking in Belgium? Certainly not Belgians). It was brilliant. To begin with, we had to retrace some of our steps from last night, which seemed counter-intuitive, but then we started walking along an old railway line which yielded a number of experiences we would otherwise have missed.

Along the way were two plaques telling us of British soldiers who won VCs in those locations.

The first, Frederick Dancox, won his medal for creeping up on a German blockhouse and taking 40 prisoners single-handed. He also carried off the German machine gun that had caused numerous British casualties. Private Dancox was given leave to receive his medal from the king and his family waited at Worcester station for his arrival, unaware that he had been killed that same day near Cambrai.

The second, Thomas Whitham from Burnley, just up the road from Hebden Bridge, took out a German machine gun and its crew after creeping from one shellhole to another while under bombardment from a British creeping barrage. Sadly, his end was a bit more prosaic: he died as a result of a post-war bicycle accident.

But, as ever, it was hard to look across that farmer's field and imagine such a scene. No shellholes now - apart from the occasional pond - just a horse staring at us curiously.

Keeping an eye on our online WW1 maps, Nick mentioned that the area to our left had been known as Battery Wood. Fiona, whose grandfather once manned a rail-mounted gun battery, pointed out that behind a fence at the bottom of the disused railway line, in the gap alongside a farm building, were some rails. The track extended for some distance through the trees beside the building, which was odd as the rails had long since been removed from the bed of the passenger railway we were walking along.

Further on was a memorial to veterans from Brittany who were overcome by the first gas attack by the Germans on April 22 1915. It was a horrific attack - but, of course, the British joined in with chemical warfare shortly afterwards.

Francis Ledwidge was one of many poets killed during the war and a monument nearby marked the spot where he died and was temporarily buried. His body was later moved a few hundred yards to Artillery Wood cemetery - astonishingly, the first British cemetery we have seen on this walk.

This railway path took us through Langemark and - serendipity again - we came across the Harry Patch memorial. Harry was the last man alive to have fought on the Western Front when he unveiled a plaque in 2008, to mark the exact spot where he crossed a brook in the Third Battle of Ypres (otherwise known as Passchendaele). Harry, who was fiercely anti-war, died the following year aged 111.

On past Pilckem, where we struggled to discern the "Ridge" that was fought so hard for, then on to Boezinghe, where we joined the canal towpath.

Halfway to Ieper is Essex Farm, where Canadian doctor John McCrae wrote one of the war's most famous poems, In Flanders Fields, probably while he waited in an ambulance. His poem, that made him something of a celebrity during the war, is engraved on a stone. The remains of the dressing station are still there, and adjoining it is the first British cemetery (no doubt the first of many) that we visited on this trip.

As well as many men from Yorkshire, it also contains the grave of the youngest British soldier to have died in the Great War: Valentine Strudwick, who was just 15.

Ieper (known as Wipers to the British soldiers) was a welcome sight, even though today was not a long day of walking. It was good to sit in the cosmopolitan square in the sunshine and order a beer.

Look at any pictures of Ypres at the end of the First World War and you will see little but piles of rubble. The houses and shops were rebuilt first, to bring the town back to life, and the public buildings later.

Thus it was that the magnificent 13th century Cloth Hall was meticulously rebuilt over a long period – and not finished until 1967. You would never know from looking at it that any of the building dated from the 20th century. Sitting outside a café in the sunshine, it has to be said: the weather is amazing. When we decided that we would keep an eye on the weather forecast after last weekend to decide when to cross to Belgium, we couldn't have guessed how lovely it was going to be.

We've had no problems with our feet, but Nick has had a little sunburn. Our original plan was to take no sun screen, to save weight, but to wait until we needed it. Well, Nick got slightly burnt on his face on Monday so wore a hat yesterday - but still got a bit burnt on his arms.

Sunburnt! In April! In northern Europe!

From a weather point of view, this is a great start - but we are fully prepared for it to go downhill in future.

Tonight, though, we are comfortable in a wonderful apartment, which allowed us to cook for ourselves. We are going to be eating in a lot of restaurants over the next few weeks, so it is a treat to prepare a simple dinner.

One of Nick's brothers questioned the wisdom of us telling everyone of our plans to do this walk. "Won't it be a bit embarrassing if you have to give up after three days?"

We are now three days in, so that line has been crossed. Let's see if we can make it to four days.

Tribute to a fallen gunner

On this day: Fierce fighting for Hill 60, near Ypres.

Day Four: Ieper to Mesen (Messines)
Miles today: 11
Total miles: 51.5

It was only last week that we discovered that Fiona's aunt Audrey had a grandfather who died and was buried on the Western Front.

Not only that, but his burial spot is close to the route we were planning for today. So our first job was to find a florist in Ieper. Astonishingly, given the number of cemeteries in the area, it turns out that there is only one florist in the town. And by a lucky chance his shop happened to be on our route too.

So lovely florist Danny prepared us a small bouquet and we fixed it to the back of Fiona's rucksack for this morning's walk.

Again, it was a glorious day and we reached the Klein-Vierstraat military cemetery after an easy walk. Belgians, as we might have suggested already, are not keen on walking but love cycling - so following the separate cycle path alongside a minor road allows for good progress.

We have been following our online trench maps and most wartime features have totally vanished. But sometimes, guided by the old maps, it's still possible to make out old trenches that haven't been completely levelled out, like the grassy fissure we spotted between two folds of a field.

In common with all Commonwealth War Graves Commission cemeteries, Klein-Vierstraat is immaculately kept. Dating from

1917/18, it includes the graves of many artillerymen, including Audrey's grandfather.

He was older than most, at 42, and the inscription on his gravestone said that he was missed by his wife and three daughters.

Early on in the war it was decided – to the disappointment of those able to afford to do so - that no bodies would be repatriated and that all war dead would be buried in some corner of a foreign field.

It was also decided, in a possibly unlikely show of egalitarianism for the time, that every man – officer or other rank, identified or not - should have the same slab of stone to mark his grave. The one allowed distinction that was offered to families was the opportunity to select an epitaph of up to 66 characters, including spaces.

But this wasn't free. Each letter cost 3.5 old pence, up to a maximum of £1. This would have been a considerable sum at the time, so many families decided against it.

The fact that Audrey's widowed grandmother chose a lengthy message for her husband's grave – and the associated cost - is still remembered by the family. As a miner's widow with three children, that must have been money she could ill afford. The message was disappointingly mundane, but it was no doubt heartfelt: "Loved and remembered by his wife and three daughters."

The least we could do was to mark her sacrifice with flowers, and Fiona laid the bouquet on his grave, then left a message in the cemetery's visitor's book.

After a picnic we set off towards the ridge we had seen this morning: the infamous Messines Ridge. It was along this ridge on June 7 1917 that the Royal Engineers detonated a series of 19 mines that tunnellers had been preparing since the previous year.

The explosions were so massive that they were heard as far away as Dublin.

This was the first time we had climbed a proper hill on our walk - not what the people of Calder Valley would call a hill, admittedly, but a real slope nevertheless. You could see why the Germans were keen to hold it.

But after the mines went off they were unable to do so. They were overrun in villages such as Witschaete, where we sat and drank lemonade under the shade of a cafe umbrella. We were sure the British troops who took the village, even in the early hours of the morning, would have preferred something stronger.

We walked on to Messines (Mesen), and the sight of WW1 barbed wire stakes being used by modern farmers to hold wire to keep livestock in check made us think of the so-called "harvest" of wartime ordnance. We haven't seen anything like that yet, but that's not to say we haven't noticed metal waste at the roadside.

It seems you can't walk 100 metres in Belgium without finding a beer can discarded from some passing car or truck.

We are spending tonight in Mesen, in a beautiful converted convent, hosted by a lovely couple who, it turns out, have been working night and day since buying it two months ago to reopen their B&B this week.

So far we have been very lucky with accommodation. The first two nights we were the only guests in the places we were staying - and we would have been again tonight if a French businessman hadn't arrived on a last-minute booking.

We had assumed we would find somewhere to eat in Mesen, but apparently not. So our hostess offered to make us, and the Frenchman, a spaghetti. Just what we needed. Let's hope we are as lucky everywhere we go.

It goes against our nature to plan too far ahead, but we are already looking out for anywhere that might be open in Béthune on Sunday night.

Giving peace a chance

On this day: Russian troops arrive at Marseille.

Day Five: Mesen to Armentières
Miles today: 10
Total miles: 61.5

Today was all about peace. Which is not something that is easy to imagine when we are constantly reminded of death and destruction.

Yesterday we missed out on the pool of peace – a lake created in one of the craters on the Messines Ridge – but today we began at the Island of Ireland Peace Park, just outside Mesen (Messines). This was opened in 1998 and commemorates the fact that Catholics and Protestants from Ireland fought alongside each other in this sector.

Poignant inscriptions are carved into stone panels, including poetry by Francis Ledwidge, whose death we read about a couple of days ago. There is also an information board with a picture of a rather glum-looking Queen alongside former Irish president Mary Robinson at the park's opening.

From there we walked on to the Christmas Truce memorial. This was in two parts: first a cross and an information board with a sketch map by soldier-cartoonist Bruce Bairnsfather, describing how he and soldiers from both sides fraternised in the field in front of us on December 25 1914.

Bairnsfather is best remembered for his cartoon character Old Bill, famously pictured in a muddy shell hole with missiles whizzing around and saying to another soldier: "Well, if you knows of a better 'ole, go to it." A short distance down the road is another memorial, complete with trench reconstructions, this time funded by UEFA – commemorating the fact that the two warring sides were brought together by football. A peace message from former UEFA president Michel Platini was translated in several languages. The memorial – an iron ball on top of a shell – is decorated with footballs, shirts and scarves (including one from Bradford City).

On that Christmas Day in 1914, Captain Robert Hamilton of the Royal Warwickshire Regiment, left his revolver behind as he climbed out of his trench and walked forward to shake the hand of a German officer of the 134th Saxon Corps.

Captain Hamilton described the event as "a day unique in the world's history". Lieutenant Kurt Zehmisch wrote in his diary that "one of the British brought a football from his trench and a vigorous football match kicked off. It was all so marvellous, so strange."

Apparently, the Germans won 3-2. Some things never change.

Beside the memorial is Prowse Point Cemetery, where we sought shelter from the sun under a tree. This is an "open

cemetery", where burials are still taking place as bodies are found, as we could see from the uneven ground and grass in front of some of the gravestones. It was a peaceful spot – until a couple of minibuses full of New Zealanders arrived. Many New Zealanders and Australians died in this area, and there was a major New Zealand memorial in Mesen.

We walked past Mud Corner and into Ploegsteert Wood (Plugstreet to the troops). No cars or buses are allowed in here and again we found peace in the three cemeteries located deep among the trees. The only sound was the birdsong. Retracing our steps to the track, we passed a party of French schoolchildren whose teacher was pointing out the trench lines in the wood and reminding them that some of the young men who died here were scarcely older than them.

The track took us to the grandiose circular Ploegsteert Memorial to the Missing at a location once known as Hyde Park Corner (many of the trenches here had London names).

More than 11,000 men with no known grave are commemorated here, and the cards and wreaths left beneath some of the panels showed that many were still remembered on the centenary of their deaths.

We stopped for a cold drink at the restaurant opposite, but resisted the temptation to have lunch, as a large group of Kiwi servicemen were doing. Instead we ate our sandwiches in the grounds of the Plugstreet 14-18 museum. If we stopped at every museum we passed on this walk we would never get anywhere, but we were tempted into this one, hidden under the ground, and it was excellent. We were particularly impressed by its accounts and pictures of the Belgian civilians displaced by the war. As we left, Fiona contributed a message of peace.

Our walk returned to the main road, heading for Armentières, and in Le Bizet – halfway along a high street – we passed into France. No big indication these days of leaving one country and moving into another, of course – just the Armentières town sign and an old customs building on the corner. By this time we were flagging in the hot sunshine, so we were glad to find our hotel and go for a beer. People of a certain age will remember that Armentières is where the mademoiselle came from:

Mademoiselle from Armentières,
Parlez-vous,
Mademoiselle from Armentières,
She hasn't been kissed for 40 years,
Hinky-dinky parlez-vous…

Like everywhere else in the area it was rebuilt after the war, so holds some interest from an art nouveau point of view, but there is little of antiquity. Ours is a typical French town hotel…typical until recently, at least. The young receptionist showed us to our room – the enormous Napoleon Suite, with a huge bathroom – and said the whole place is being refurbished after the retirement of her grandmother.

We both knew as she said it that if we were to return in a year, the old furniture will be gone and everything will be painted grey. Except for the bits that are lime green or purple.

Hidden signs of a violent past

On this day 1918: German airman Captain von Richthofen was killed.

Day Six: Armentières to Richebourg
Miles today: 14.5
Total miles: 76

We crisscrossed the two sides' front lines today. Not that we would have known that if we hadn't had a set of old trench maps on our tablet.

The fields on each side of the roads we walked looked peaceful and well-kept. It was only the creeping cursor on our screen that told us we were walking alongside the old Allied front line or moving across No Man's Land and into what was once German-held territory.

Again we were amused by the names given to trenches and features by the British mapmakers. On one side of a road we walked this morning there was a trench called Safety Alley. On the other side of the road, nearer enemy lines, the trench was called Queer Street.

No prizes for guessing which side the British troops preferred.

At the end of the road where we are staying tonight is Chocolate Menier Corner - named after an advert once painted on the side of a house there. Stretching back from it are trenches called Cadbury and Fry. And towards the end of today's walk we were running parallel with Black Adder trench.

The war, of course, was appalling for all participants. But our thoughts keep returning to the most innocent victims: the local residents whose whole lives were turned upside-down by the conflict. As we walked along this morning, we wondered what the local farmers said when troops started digging trenches across their fields. Yesterday, at the Plugstreet 14-18 museum, we saw many pictures of the refugees trudging away with their few possessions. For many, it was to be 10 years or more before they were able to return to their homes.

Others had to stay and work with the invaders - whether they wanted to or not. And, of course, many lost their lives as their homes were shelled.

A war memorial brought this home to us this afternoon when we took a break in Aubers. Three sides of the memorial bore the names of soldiers from that parish who had died in wars. The rear of the memorial listed all the 14-18 civilians.

But now all is calm and peace - though we were reminded again early today by a plaque on a wall recalling a Nazi execution that the First World War was not the only conflict to affect this region. There was little to see to mark the devastation once caused to this area so it was almost a surprise, when walking down some quiet lanes, to come across two German bunkers - one with steps leading inside, though none too invitingly.

When we planned this walk, we decided to keep an eye on the weather from the middle of April and get started if the forecast was reasonable. There is no way we could have anticipated/hoped for the weather we have had this week. The last few days we have been walking in the sort of heat we thought we would not encounter until July. It has been good - but it is also tiring. At around lunchtime we arrived in the village of Fromelles, hoping to find a café. Once every French village had at least one café but, disappointingly, so many have closed down. The one in Fromelles, miraculously, had been converted to a rather posh wine shop and bar, and restaurant. We entered, feeling a bit sweaty and grubby, and were offered stools at the bar.

The only other customers were some rather monosyllabic elderly Australians who arrived for lunch and ate outside. Inside, to the music of the Rolling Stones, we first drank lemon and lime, then, feeling refreshed, decided to go for a beer too. The staff were charming and offered slices of sausage. It was tempting to stay and eat more.

But we had a sandwich in our rucksacks, so we went back out into the heat and shared it in the shade of the porch of the Pheasant Wood military cemetery. We hadn't planned to come here, but it turns out it has an unusual story.

Fromelles was the scene of a diversionary attack during the Battle of the Somme, further south, in July 1916. Many Australian troops were involved and, of course, many became casualties.

The cemetery was inaugurated only in 2010 after two mass graves were excavated in a nearby wood. Attempts were made to identify as many as possible, using medical records and the DNA of descendants of missing soldiers. Inevitably, many are still unidentified, but a large number now have names.

It was the first new Commonwealth military cemetery built since the 1960s and there is still plenty of room - presumably to allow for future discoveries.

Talking of diversions, later we walked past a lane - after passing through Aubers and Neuve-Chapelle - with a plaque at its end. It told the story of an ill-fated, and no doubt ill-advised, effort by British commanders to confuse the Germans on the eve of the Battle of the Somme. A pals' battalion from Sussex was sent in to fight the Germans at a spot called the Boar's Head (named after the shape of the front line). The Germans weren't fooled.

Hundreds of young men were killed in a few hours - leading June 30 to be dubbed "the day Sussex died".

Today was a longer walk than the last few days. We've been trying not to overdo it in our first week and we've been using the internet to book accommodation in advance.

This has been a blessing and a slight curse. A curse only because it removes the spontaneity, and also because it makes it less likely that we will find accommodation that isn't on sites such as booking.com.

But it's essential to know we have a bed for the night, and tonight we are in a comfortable converted stable block where we were able to wash all our grubby clothes and cook for ourselves again. Our host offered to drive us to a shop to buy dinner, which was kind of him, but we recoiled from the idea of getting into a car.

Luckily, we had come prepared. Our email asking if there was a restaurant nearby assured us that there was – five kilometres away. A 10km round trip walk to dinner was obviously out of the question, so we had carried our dinner with us all day in the heat. Including a bottle of wine.

Tomorrow should be a short walk, if only because we thought we were more likely to find food on a Sunday evening if we were in a bigger town. But we don't know (it's easy to get obsessed with thoughts of where our next dinner is coming from). Yesterday was a short walk as the crow flies - but that allowed us to do a bit of sightseeing.

Let's see what tomorrow brings.

A sunny Sunday morning stroll

ON THIS DAY 1915: Second Battle of Ypres begins: town of Ypres largely destroyed; German advance checked by Canadians after French retreat before poisonous gas attack.

Day Seven: Richebourg to Béthune
Miles today: 9
Total miles: 85

Seven days in, and it's a sunny Sunday afternoon in Béthune. We had wondered if we would want days off from walking, but so far we've reckoned that it was better to keep moving forward.

Today was a short walk anyway, dictated by practicality. Most restaurants are closed in France on a Sunday night, so we decided we would stand the best chance of eating tonight if we were in a town. We might otherwise have skirted round Béthune.

We had no expectations of a town in the industrial zone of northern France so were surprised to find a charming square. And for the first time we have seen buildings that predate the 1920s.

This morning's short walk means we were installed in our hotel room overlooking the Grand'Place by early afternoon. Time for a Sunday rest after a stroll around and an ice cream.

Today's walk began in peaceful countryside, but we are resigned to the fact that the next two days we will be walking two sides of the Béthune-Lens-Arras industrial triangle.

We'll try to make it as scenic as possible and - ever the optimists - are prepared to be pleasantly surprised. We'll see.

After Arras on Wednesday morning, we shall be heading out into open country again and towards the Somme. But today's countryside was pleasant enough, though sadly lacking in shade on a very hot April day.

Fiona's hips make it difficult for her to sit on the ground, so we are in trouble if we don't find a bench, a wall, or something similar to perch on. And today we really felt we needed to get out of the sun.

Our wartime maps told us we were walking past a one-time Indian camp at one point. This must have seemed a very alien place to men uprooted from the Indian sub-continent and dropped down here to fight the Germans.

As we approached Béthune, we began to catch the aroma of Sunday lunches wafting out of kitchen windows, which was tantalising. No matter – we had a slap-up lunch of our own. We dodged an industrial zone by finding a walkers' and cyclists' path alongside a stretch of old canal and a dock, where we sat on a bench under a tree and enjoyed our banana sandwiches.

As we sheltered from the heat, we texted our daughters, who were horrified to hear what we were eating... but two pieces of baguette and a banana were all we had managed to salvage from this morning's breakfast, and there were no shops anywhere. So there it was: banana sandwiches, the lunch of kings.

And now, we're going to mention trekking poles. It's possible that if you haven't tried them, you think they are a bit wussy. Nick did (though Fiona had tried them out to take the weight - not that there is much, of course - off her bad hips). Now we are both converts.

They are especially good if you are carrying a pack as they take the weight off your feet. They spread some of the walking effort to your arms, reducing the effort of your legs and giving your upper body a bit of a workout.

They are also helpful on slopes (not that we've seen many yet) and give added stability on uneven ground.

Nick is very grateful to former colleague and keen walker Peter Beal, who said we really ought to use poles. Of course, technique is crucial, and there are some unintentionally amusing videos on YouTube to make sure you get it right ("DON'T USE THE DEATH GRIP!!"). But once you get into a rhythm, it turns out trekking poles are the best thing since Compeed.

My boy Jack…we found him

On this day 1916: British bombard Belgian coast.

Day Eight: Béthune to Lens
Miles today: 14.5
Total miles: 99.5

Rudyard Kipling was desperately keen for his only son to do his "patriotic" duty and serve in the First World War. So keen that when John's eyesight ruled him out of both the navy and the army, he pulled some strings.

He spoke to his friend Lord Roberts, former commander-in-chief of the British army, and John was given a commission as a second lieutenant shortly after his 17th birthday.

He went to France where, during the Battle of Loos in 1915, he was shot in the head. He was just 18.

John was reported missing and his grief-stricken father went to enormous lengths to find him, even touring the Western Front himself as the war continued and arranging for leaflets to be dropped behind German lines. Eventually he was convinced that his son was dead, and he wrote the poem My Boy Jack (which seems, curiously, to be more appropriate to a son who had been in the navy):

"Have you news of my boy Jack?"
Not this tide.
"When d'you think that he'll come back?"
Not with this wind blowing, and this tide.

"Has any one else had word of him?"
Not this tide.

For what is sunk will hardly swim,
Not with this wind blowing, and this tide.

"Oh, dear, what comfort can I find?"
None this tide, Nor any tide,
Except he did not shame his kind -
Not even with that wind blowing, and that tide.
Then hold your head up all the more,
This tide,
And every tide;
Because he was the son you bore,
And gave to that wind blowing and that tide!

His son's death didn't turn Kipling against war - in fact, his
hatred of Germans became even more intense - but it did motivate
him to get involved in the Imperial (now Commonwealth) War
Graves Commission. It was Kipling who suggested the words
"Their name liveth for ever more" that appear in every
Commonwealth war cemetery.

He also proposed the words "A soldier of the Great War known
unto God" on the gravestones of unidentified remains... such as
those of his own son.

Kipling never did find his son's grave as it wasn't identified until 1992 (and even then it was a controversial identification). But we found it, by chance, this morning at the St Mary's ADS cemetery (ADS for advance dressing station and St Mary's because most of the medical staff there trained at St Mary's hospital in Paddington, London, where our first daughter was born) on the road from Vermelles to Hulluch.

We started earlier today as, for the first time, we were staying somewhere with no breakfast provided. Béthune was getting off to a slow Monday morning start as we walked the long road out of town.

After calling in at a boulangerie to stock up with breakfast and lunch, we witnessed a scene that could have come out of a classic French comedy film. Two workmen, whose "Route barrée" (road closed) sign had been ignored by Monday morning commuters, attempted to block the road with a moveable fence.

As they moved it to the left, the waiting cars passed it on the right. As they slid it back again, they nipped past on the left. And meanwhile, more and more cars were ignoring the sign and impatiently joining the traffic jam.

We trekked out of town down a long main road, stopping at a Lidl to stock up on chocolate and then at a slightly grubby café for hot drinks to go with our breakfast pastries.

Eventually we were able to turn off that main road, making good progress in the cooler weather. For the first time in six days we were wearing long sleeves, and there was a refreshing breeze.

Soon the slagheaps of the old coalfields came into view. If the heatwave had continued today, it would have felt even more like walking towards the pyramids at Giza.

Then we saw the cemeteries. Cemeteries plural, as there were three side by side.

We visited John Kipling, if that's who it is, whose grave was marked by a poppy wreath from the Kipling Society. The other two cemeteries were up a track. One was a tiny one, just 45 men buried in what was once a shell crater.

In the other, we stopped for our sandwich lunch, sheltering by the wall from the breeze and listening to the skylarks overhead.

The original plan had been to take the main road into Lens, but we realised that the farm track we were on led towards Loos. So we walked along it between potato fields, following the course of an old trench.

Loos - the town whose name was lent to an epic battle - is now a quiet suburb, but of course most such places are. We wondered what it must be like to live in a place with such a notorious name, a name that would be recognised by anyone who asked and immediately linked to violent historical events.

The road led us up a slope, past the Loos war cemetery, where we stopped again for a rest. Three thousand graves... including some RAF men from the Second World War.

As we walked into Lens we were reminded that we were at the heart of the old coalfields. Estates of pit cottages - marked as "cities" on the map with roads laid out on a grid system - flanked our route, though, oddly, the two biggest slagheaps were no longer visible.

History has not been kind to Lens: smashed in the First World War, bombed heavily in the Second. And despite an impressive stadium, its football team is languishing in Ligue 2.

But we received a friendly welcome from tonight's youthful hotel owner. She was impressed by our effort - but topped it with the story of last week's guest: a truck driver in his 50s who decided to use his legs at last and stayed here when he was 200km into a 2,400km walk.

We'd better keep walking.

Vimy Ridge: it's hidden behind Arras

On this day 1916: Zeppelin raid on Norfolk and Suffolk coast – one killed, one injured.

Day Nine: Lens to Arras
Miles today: 15
Total miles: 114.5

As soon as we turned off the long, straight, stragglingly urban road heading out of Lens, we saw it. Suddenly we were in the country, and ahead of us was the brilliant white monument pointing to the sky from the top of Vimy Ridge.

By this time we were feeling chilly. The T-shirts of two days ago had been covered up by long sleeves, and as the cold wind blew in our faces, we stopped to put on rain jackets. Not that it rained, though it threatened to, but we needed to cheat the wind.

By the time we reached the village of Givenchy-en-Gohelle, at the foot of the ridge, we needed to stop for hot chocolate. Although the village had been decked out in Canadian flags ever since last year's centenary of the capture of the Ridge by Canadian forces, there were no tourists in the village café. It was 11am and the women were drinking coffee at the tables, the men were already on the beer at the bar.

Up the hill, the steepest yet on our walk, and we emerged on to the plateau that is the Canadian memorial park. It's dominated on one side by the massive monument in white stone that commemorates the Canadians with no known grave. On the other is woodland, where the shell holes and mine craters have never been smoothed over. This is one place where you take notice of the "Do not walk on the grass" signs. They warn of unexploded bombs under the trees, which should be enough to put off the curious, even without the electric fences.

As we approached the monument, which dominates the coal-producing plain in front of it, we heard the sound of young people behind us and turned to see a coachload of teenagers. Where were they from, we asked one of the teachers. All over, he replied - they were from the international school in Brno, in the Czech Republic.

Any Canadians? Yes, actually both he and his fellow teacher were Canadians. And, wouldn't you know it, his family were from Hamilton, Ontario, where Fiona's sister and brother-in-law live. Small world.

After a close look at the monument, we walked through the trees towards the Canadian visitor centre, built since we first visited the ridge with our daughters 20 years ago, and one question was answered for us.

How do they keep the grass trim if it's dangerous to walk on the pitted ground? They use sheep, of course.

A Canadian couple stopped with us to gaze at the sheep. Did they know their job was so dangerous, we wondered.

Sadly, few other questions were answered as the visitor centre - still looking pretty new - was closed for the week for "essential

maintenance". But we wandered over to the preserved trenches, which look even more sanitised (with their concrete sandbags and gravelled floors) than we remembered them.

The best part of the visit is the guided tour of the tunnels, which shouldn't be missed, but we had done that before on that previous visit so we began the walk down the hill.

We stopped to eat our sandwiches in Neuville-Saint-Vaast, a village that saw ferocious fighting from cellar to cellar in 1917 but which, like so many places, was rebuilt after the war.

We could have visited the largest German war cemetery in France, but today was not a day of cemetery visits - and anyway we preferred to take the quiet route to Arras, avoiding the main road.

We looked back and, oddly, the Vimy memorial was nowhere to be seen. How could something so dominant on one side of the ridge have become so invisible from the other?

We walked on, aware that we were crossing old trenches and railway lines but seeing nothing but vast fields. We entered Arras, and what a difference from Lens. The town suffered terribly in both wars but here the architectural gems - the squares, the belltower, the town hall - have been faithfully reproduced, as in Ieper, and it is almost impossible to tell the difference.

We sat in the Place des Héros, surrounded by perfectly rebuilt Flemish baroque townhouses, and enjoyed a beer.

Arras is a lovely town. We want to come back and see more – especially the network of quarry tunnels that were used to shelter soldiers during the First World War.

The long and windy road

Day 10: Arras to Auchonvillers
Miles today: 19
Total miles: 133.5

The Somme. There are few regions of the world whose name resonates so profoundly in the English-speaking nations.

July 1 1916, first day of the Battle of the Somme, is still the worst day for casualties in British military history - 60,000 men dead or wounded. Tonight we are sleeping close to the British front line on the Somme battlefields in a house built on top of an old cellar that was once a dressing station for injured troops.

Avril Williams has run her B&B and tea room at Auchonvillers - Ocean Villas to the Tommies - since the early 1990s, and this is our second visit. We were last here with our girls in about 1995, though on that occasion we came just for afternoon tea. It was a memorable visit as Avril took us down into the cellar, whose walls are covered in graffiti and the marks left by rifles fitted with bayonets stacked in the corner. Avril was able to identify the authors of some of those graffiti - sometimes only by reference to lists of the war dead. I wrote about that candle-lit visit in a battlefield tourism feature for a Yorkshire Post WW1 souvenir issue.

Sadly, the cellar is no longer open to visits as too many people have fallen on the steep stairs, but Avril says she has plans to make it more accessible in the future. There is still plenty to see: a trench behind the house has been excavated, and Avril has been buying up collections of war memorabilia and has promised to show us round tomorrow. Her museum has come on a long way since her son Mark showed us his own collection of wartime finds that he kept in the barn all those years ago.

Today was our longest walk yet, and it would have been a good one if it hadn't been for the weather. After some heavy cloud early on, it actually became quite fine - but there was a strong wind. At no point was the wind in our favour, so it was often heavy going.

We left behind the suburbs of Arras on a minor road that became a farm track, crossing first the British front line, then the German. We were supposed to be taking the road after that, but Nick couldn't resist a track called the Chemin des Morts (Way of the Dead). It threatened to peter out completely but continued on between potato fields and eventually led us back to a road – to our relief as we didn't fancy having to retrace our steps.

The fields are huge here and show little sign of having hosted one of the most violent episodes in world history, but our trench maps told us we were passing through an area where a whole alternative "civilisation" had once sprung up. Not just trenches, but also railway lines, tramways, camps, supply dumps. All now wiped away. There was little sign of life in any of the villages we passed - not a cafe or a shop - and we ate our sandwich in a village bus shelter in the absence of a bench.

As we walked into the Somme battle area, we followed the trench lines on our maps. We looked left and saw Gommecourt Wood not far away from the road, one front line to the other, giving us an idea of just how narrow No Man's Land was at some points.

Buffeted by the wind, we finally made it to Auchonvillers, a beer, and a chat with Avril. As we all ate dinner around a long table – shepherd's pie, possibly the only time we will eat that during this trip - our evening was made livelier by the arrival of a jolly cycling group from Suffolk, who turned up a bit late as they had also felt the effects of the wind. One chap told us he had been a member of the group since 1957. Seems we are not the oldest people on the Western Front trail.

A walk through No Man's Land

On this day 1915: British airmen bomb Courtrai and neighbouring towns.

Day 11: Auchonvillers to Albert
Miles today: 11.5
Total miles: 145

In the heart of the Somme we had to do some sightseeing. And we started at the guesthouse where we spent the night.

Avril Williams moved to the Somme to open a B&B in the early 1990s. She had no particular interest in the First World War, but it gradually took over her life. Now she is expanding her B&B with new apartments, her tearoom is constantly busy with coach parties of battlefield tourists - and her home has become a destination in itself.

Not only is the house full of wartime memorabilia, but her garden has been excavated to reveal the original trench system that led to the advance dressing station in her cellar. Across the road, she has created a meeting hall/conference centre out of an old cowshed, and next to that is almost certainly the best private WW1 (and WW2) museum in France.

Avril showed us round, pointing out the most interesting exhibits, and telling tales about foolish tourists who pick up old shells by the side of the road, or even buy them. One person's "souvenir" was discovered in his luggage in Paris, resulting in the evacuation of the Gare du Nord, while another made the fatal mistake of putting a leaky mustard gas shell in his boot... The war ended nearly 100 years ago, but these things are still dangerous. Avril's guesthouse is a one-off and so is she. Highly recommended if you are planning a visit to the Somme. From "Ocean Villas". we walked down the Beaumont Road, crossing the old British front line into No Man's Land. The footage of the massive mine blowing up underneath the German front line on Hawthorn Ridge just before 7.30am on the first day of the Battle of the Somme is probably the most famous moving image of the entire war – and this is where it was filmed by Geoffrey Malins.

We walked up the sunken road in No Man's Land where soldiers from Lancashire waited in the early hours to go over the top. When day broke, they were spotted by the Germans and shelled - and few got very far after leaving the road.

Walking up the steep slope towards the German lines (as so many attempted to do but so few succeeded) it is now possible to visit the Hawthorn mine crater. It is being cleared of the trees and bushes that have filled it for years, and its depth and width are powerful evidence of the enormous blast that took place here.

Blowing the mine – with its 18,000kg of explosive – was the first action of the battle, timed to go off 10 minutes before the attack to allow British troops to shelter from the falling debris. This proved to be a mistake: although many German soldiers were killed, it gave others time to regroup and fire at the attackers coming up the hill.

We decided to give the Newfoundland Park a miss as we had visited it before, but it should be high on the list of any first-time visitor to the area. The sector where so many Newfoundlanders died is preserved forever, grassed over but still a memorial to the many men who were mown down even before they were able to get to their frontline trench on July 1 1916.

Although softened by time, the trench system is still clear and you can walk through the front-line trench that was once so full of casualties that troops had to emerge from trenches to the rear – making them easy targets for German machine-gunners. Nowadays you can walk easily from one front line to the other. It's only a short walk. Halfway across No Man's Land is a replica of the Danger Tree. Very few Newfies got past that point, let alone to the German wire. Moving behind the old German front line we crossed the now-peaceful River Ancre and took a field track to the Ulster Tower, which commemorates the advances made on the first day by the troops from Ulster - sadly in vain.

This position again demonstrates how close the two sides were. The track – past the heavily-fortified Schwaben Redoubt on the German front line – seems to be no distance from the edge of Thiepval Wood, where the Ulstermen emerged from trenches into ferocious gunfire.

Against the odds, the men from Ulster advanced as far as the German fifth line, where they waited for support. It failed to arrive and by the time they were withdrawn, they had suffered 5,500 casualties, including 2,000 dead.

So this land is very special to the people of Northern Ireland and the Ulster Tower, a copy of Helen's Tower on the Clandeboye Estate, in Co Down, is the province's national war memorial. This week has included Anzac Day, so we have seen a lot of Aussies touring the battlefields. There was a busload of them at the Ulster Tower, where it was both reassuring and disorientating to hear Ulster accents.

Phoebe and Teddy have been running the café and visitor centre since 2001. He is now in his 80s and she is not far behind, but they seemed run off their feet. A newspaper cutting on the wall recorded their "final retirement" last year, but they were still there. We were rather envious of them living up the tower... sadly, applications for their job closed the day before.

A couple from Northern Ireland were helping them out as volunteers ("we're on holiday" - but it didn't look much like a holiday). She was serving teas and sandwiches, while he alternated between fixing the terrace outside and handing out shrapnel balls from a bucket to visitors ("you find millions of them in the fields, so you do... but make sure you don't put them in your hand luggage when you fly home").

We walked on up to Thiepval, where Lutyens's monstrous hilltop monument looms over the area. It's on the site of the original Thiepval chateau and commemorates the missing of the

Somme. Its panels display around 72,000 names, which is always hard to take in – and that is just the missing British and Commonwealth soldiers. It cannot be described as pretty, but it is definitely monumental.

It was here that Nick met several centenarian Somme veterans when he attended the 80th anniversary commemorations on July 1 1996. One of those men told him that he was in France on the first day of the First World War, went over the top on the afternoon of the first day of the Battle of the Somme, and was still serving in the British army when the war ended. It seems some people are just born lucky.

Underneath the arch, shivering in a fleece (we were on a ridge and there was a cool breeze), was a young man who stepped forward to greet us. He looked like he might be about to invite us to sign up for a charity standing order, but he turned out to be an intern for the Commonwealth War Graves Commission. Despite the coolness, there are no doubt worse places to be an intern.

In front of the memorial is a shared cemetery – one side is made up of British Portland stone slabs, while the other half is French concrete crosses. The French Tricolore and the Union flag both fly here. It's a potent symbol of unity – the bodies of the men who fought together under different flags now lying together. But today we weren't tempted to linger. Turning our backs on the monument, we strolled along farm tracks to Albert, making today a fairly relaxed day of walking.

In Albert we admired the golden virgin on top of the rebuilt basilica. This was one of the most famous symbols of the war – and an excellent target for artillery. It was believed by British troops that the war would end when the original virgin finally fell. For years she hung on, leaning at a perilous angle.

She was eventually toppled by British gunners during the German spring offensive of 1918 - but the war took seven months longer to come to an end.

Evidence from the killing fields

On this day 1917: French offensive on the Aisne checked.

Day 12: Albert to Péronne
Miles today: 16
Total miles: 161

Today we walked across some of the worst killing fields in the history of mankind. Of course, you would never guess that to look at the wide open spaces under a blue sky with great fluffy clouds.

But two things give it away. First, of course, the cemeteries. As we left Albert, we passed the huge French cemetery, with its concrete crosses back to back - one field, 6,000 dead.

In Fricourt, where we stopped to eat our late breakfast from the boulangerie in Albert, we passed a graveyard full of pals from West Yorkshire who all died on the same day: July 1 1916. Just up the road was the German cemetery with its 17,000 bodies.

The First World War truly was a bloody disaster for the youth of Europe. And for all the other countries around the world that were dragged into this imperial conflict.

From Fricourt to Mametz and beyond, we were following the old roads - now farm tracks, bypassed by modern traffic - that our grandfathers might have marched along to the front.

Walking there, crossing and recrossing old front lines, it is hard not to keep looking at the edges of those fields that are still bare for evidence of the war - and if you look hard enough, it is there. First, we spotted a shell case, tossed to the field edge, then other

bits of battle debris, such as shell nose cones. Finally, we saw an unexploded shell, placed or perhaps thrown to one side by a farmer.

One hundred years on, this stuff is still surfacing even following year after year of ploughing. Of course, dig deeper than a foot or two and this ground is still heavily polluted with the detritus of war, and always will be.

Ahead of us we saw the French and British flags, and a plaque told us we had reached the exact point where the French front line met the British sector. Someone had left some rusty old bits of wartime iron there too.

One recurring theme in any contemporary account of the war is the difference between British and French trenches. Invariably, the British troops complained when taking over French trenches that they were left in a disgraceful condition and needed a lot of tidying up. As we rounded the edge of a wood and struck out along a path across a field, we were once again reminded by our GPS and the old trench maps of just how close the allied front line was to the opposing trenches. Almost close enough here to lob something across by hand.

The 21st century intruded eventually, first as we went under the TGV line and the autoroute, and then as we reached Clery-sur-Somme and were forced to walk the last section to Péronne on the main road.

Most of the day had been a pleasure but trying to stare into the eyes of speeding drivers to force them to move around us as we trudged along wasn't much fun. A useful reminder to avoid main roads whenever possible, even if it means a slightly longer walk.

Péronne was in German hands for most of the war, being finally liberated by the Australians only in September 1918. Its medieval chateau houses a superb museum, the Historial de la Grande Guerre, but we have visited that before.

Tonight we restricted our sightseeing to a bar and then a supermarket, where we bought food to cook in our apartment. For a couple of hours, Nick was able to forget the war for a couple of hours as he watched a Fulham match live on his phone.

At least you don't have to wait four years for victory in a football match.

Goodbye to all that

Day 13: Péronne to Mesnil-St-Nicaise
Miles today: 13.5
Total miles: 174.5

As we headed south from Péronne, we felt we were leaving the worst horrors of the war behind for the time being - and, to be honest, it was a bit of a relief. But it turned out we were getting ahead of ourselves.

We were roughly following the line of the River Somme and we reached Brie mid-morning (not THAT Brie) to find a signpost to the Commonwealth war cemetery. Because Brie has a bridge over the river, which is very marshy at that point, it was a prize position that was seized from the Germans who held it.

But now we are walking away from the Somme and its battlefields - and all the Australians.

Last Wednesday was Anzac Day, commemorating the part played by the Australians and New Zealanders, so many of the battlefield tourists we have come across this week have been a long way from home.

The people of Péronne are particularly grateful to the Australians who helped to liberate their town, as evidenced by the jokey Roo de Kanga street sign we saw (and the Playmobil exhibition about Australia that we didn't see). Nick was looking at an old photo in the town that showed Australian troops standing on a pavement. He looked up and realised Fiona was standing on that exact same spot.

Tonight we are staying in a rather grand B&B in the country. We must be getting fitter because we extended today's walk with a bit of a detour to add some distance and avoid arriving too early. We said before we started that accommodation and food could make or break this expedition. We have to know where the next bed and dinner are coming from.

You can no longer count on French villages and small towns offering anything. In all our walking so far, we have probably passed two open cafés and one village shop away from the main towns - but no boulangeries, and no hotels. Many village shops and cafés have closed across France so we need to carry our lunch.

Then every few days we have to sit down with the tablet and the wifi and plan the next few nights. We get an idea of where we want to go, then, using mainly Booking.com, we see what is available. It can be a time-consuming process, and involves some compromise on routes as this ultimately has to be determined by where there are overnight vacancies and restaurants.

Weekends can be tricky as many places prefer a two-night booking - and a lot of restaurants close on Sundays. Last night we stayed in a superb aparthotel overlooking the main square in Péronne (with the bonus of wifi good enough to watch the football), and the night before in, let's say, a rather more basic studio flat. But we like being able to cook for ourselves sometimes as it makes a change from eating out. Tonight's meal was prepared for us by our hosts, who joined us for dinner - some good French home cooking, as well as excellent company. One of the pleasures of travelling like this is that we do get to meet some people along the way, and tonight reminded us that we must try to use chambres d'hôtes more when we are in France. Our hosts had created a beautiful home out of a 19th century house that they told us had once housed a brewery.

As we arrived, we were impressed to see their robot lawn-mower busying itself around the garden. Apparently they are now all the rage in France. Nick wants one.

But the best bit was the meal that was jointly cooked by our hosts. You can't march on an empty stomach.

The solitary but watery path

On this day 1917: General Pétain appointed chief of French general staff.

Day 14: Mesnil-St-Nicaise to Noyon
Miles today: 17
Total miles: 191.5

It had to happen: two weeks of walking in April, and today we had our first rain. It started as a gentle drizzle, then gradually became more persistent. And colder.

It all started so promisingly as we left last night's stop, and our hosts (and new best friends) William and Gaelle. We dined superbly with them last night and we took pictures of each other before waving goodbye after breakfasting with them too.

They had suggested walking alongside the canal today, so after a visit to Auchan supermarket in Nesle (pronounced Nell if you're wondering - as we were) to buy quiches for lunch, we headed across the fields to the towpath.

The Canal du Nord is not like a British canal - it's blooming wide for a start. It was planned in the 19th century to help the coal industry but work didn't begin until 1908. After being badly damaged in the First World War before its completion, the project was abandoned until the 1950s.

So, unlike our 18th century British canals, this one didn't even open to traffic until 1966. One suspects that was a bit too late. There was absolutely no sign of any boats.

The only people we saw on the towpath all day were two cyclists who came racing up behind us. There was one slightly nervous moment for Nick (the map-reader) as we approached a tunnel. No immediate sign of a way off the towpath, definitely no walking through the tunnel, and a long way back to the last bridge.

It was a bit of a relief, then, to find a well-disguised flight of steps right at the tunnel entrance that took us up to a track and then the road. Sometimes you just have to trust the map.

It wasn't really a day for picnicking as the rain was pretty heavy by the time we were feeling too hungry and tired to keep going. Who would have thought we would ever feel so grateful to see a village bus shelter so we could at least have a sit down (almost) out of the rain?

Looking up from the shelter, we realised we were looking at an old church. An OLD church... probably the first church we have seen in the past two weeks that wasn't rebuilt in the 1920s or 1930s. We are finally moving into an area where there are buildings that weren't totally razed between 1914 and 1918. The rebuilt church at Mesnil-St-Nicaise and the solitary Commonwealth war grave in the churchyard this morning were today's last obvious signs of that conflict.

A weary trudge into Noyon and we were delighted to discover our hotel is right next to the medieval gothic cathedral, surrounded by beautiful old houses. AND our room has a bath...bonus!

We hoped we might find somewhere open for dinner on a Sunday night, though the hotel receptionist didn't sound too hopeful. It was still raining when we went in search of food, so we weren't able to linger and appreciate the fine old buildings – including one that was General John French's HQ for a day or two before the Germans moved in.

Just as we began to fear that tonight was the night when we would have to fall back on a pizza, we saw it. A Japanese restaurant. Japanese? In a French provincial town on a Sunday night? Yup. And it was OK.

Wet, wet, wet... and frozen

On this day 1916: German attack from Messines Ridge defeated by artillery.

Day 15: Noyon to Coucy-le-Château
Miles today: 20
Total miles: 211.5

What a horrible , horrible day. We knew the weather forecast was bad - and Wet Wet Wet were on the hotel radio at breakfast - but we didn't know HOW bad it was going to be. And this was our longest walk so far.

It didn't start too badly, as the expected rain hadn't appeared by the time we left Noyon (a town we have noted down as worth a return visit). The skies looked threatening and it was a bit chilly, but this time we had taken the precaution of putting on our waterproofs and attaching the rucksack covers before we set off.

Yesterday we were fiddling around with our rucksacks on a canal towpath in the rain, trying to remember which zip on Fiona's pack was hiding the cover. Nick even had to consult a YouTube video about the rucksack. Should have checked before. Schoolboy error.

Anyway, it hadn't even started to rain after a couple of hours walking along the Canal latéral à l'Oise - not to be confused with the Sambre-Oise canal, where Wilfred Owen was killed a week before the Armistice in 1918.

We'd passed a lock where the lock-keeper waved to us from his cabin. We joked that he was probably waiting for the first boat of the year... then as we approached the bridge where we were leaving the canal, a pleasure boat, the Missing Link, motored past, giving us a toot.

And as we crossed the bridge, blow me but a proper French canal barge came looming up in the other direction.

It was when we started across country that the rain began - light to begin with but sharpening up in the atrocious wind into freezing

needles. At one point it started hailing.

Today's route would have been an excellent walk in fine weather, but this was anything but fine. The ferocious wind blew the rain right across us, and unlike yesterday - when it stopped mid-afternoon - there was no let-up.

And precious little shelter. We passed a café - closed. We tried a church door - locked.

We stood in the lee of the church fumbling with frozen fingers to extract the quilted jackets from our rucksacks to put on under our rain jackets. It was painful. Interestingly, the church had Commonwealth war graves in its yard - the burial place of seven

Second World War airmen – but we didn't feel inclined to do any sightseeing.

Finally, like yesterday, we found a bus shelter where we could eat our sandwich. No chance of eating the hardboiled eggs we liberated from this morning's breakfast buffet. Our fingers were too numb to have any chance of peeling off the shells.

Our lightweight packing has been pretty much spot-on so far, but today we desperately needed gloves - something that would have seemed laughable in the heatwave of a fortnight ago. For much of the day we trailed our trekking poles uselessly from our wrists as we tried to keep our hands in our pockets. So, little chance either of taking any more pictures. It made us wonder how soldiers standing in frozen trenches managed to pull the triggers of their rifles.

Back on the road, the walk seemed endless. The wind and rain were constant, though every so often a particularly fierce blast would threaten to blow us off our feet. A couple of times Nick had to grab Fiona's arm to stop her being blasted into a ditch.

In better weather, and with fewer miles to walk, we might have been tempted by the signs for Château de Blérancourt and its Franco-American museum. This was founded by American heiress Anne Morgan, daughter of financier JP Morgan, who left her comfortable life in the States to devote herself to relief work during and after the war in France.

She bought what remained of the devastated 17th century chateau as a base and later donated it to the local town as a museum. She was made an officer of the Legion of Honour and was later elevated to commander – one of only two women to hold that rank at the time and the first American woman to be so honoured.

In 1948 Eleanor Roosevelt visited the château and wrote: "You can still imagine how grand the old château must have been… But you also are forced to wonder all over again, as you drive in, whether we human beings are bound to go on destroying each other and our possessions forever." As we arrived in the village where we are staying, we tried using Google Maps on our phones, which was tricky. Our shivering fingers could barely touch the screens accurately enough to type out the address – and we needed to stand under the shelter of someone's overhanging roof to stop the phones getting drenched.

Cruelly, tonight's accommodation turned out to be at the top of another hill. We must have looked a right sight as we trailed up the steep slope, the gap between us growing longer and longer. When we found tonight's B&B, it was over a shop. We pushed the door open and stood there, shivering and dripping wet, half-fearing we would be driven away by an outraged shopkeeper. Instead we were given a warm welcome, provided with clothes racks and hot drinks, and made to feel human again. No bath, but a hot shower helped to restore us to something like normality.

By dinner-time we were able to make ourselves look sufficiently respectable to cross the square to a proper old-fashioned French bourgeois hotel restaurant and a proper old-fashioned French bourgeois hotel restaurant dinner.

It had stopped raining by the time we emerged - and this does look like a fascinating village. The castle at Coucy-le-Château was apparently one of the biggest and most intact medieval structures in Europe. It was occupied by the Germans from 1914, but as they left in 1917 - to universal outrage - they blew the place up.

Hooray, hooray, the First of May

On this day 1915: Second Battle of Ypres – repulse of German attack on Hill 60. British ordered to withdraw to new line.

Day 16: Coucy-le-Château to Laon
Miles today: 16
Total miles: 227.5

"Hooray, hooray, the first of May/Outdoor sex begins today." Someone said on Facebook today that they missed Nick's traditional greeting of this new month. So here it is.

Nick used to work on the gossip page of the Daily Mirror and one of its editors loved to sneak that little rhyme into the paper every year.

Outdoor sex today? Well, it was feasible, despite the damp undergrowth. What a difference a day makes.

After yesterday's fierce, freezing storm, today dawned bright and tranquil. We left Coucy-le-Château by the medieval Porte de Laon, passed the workshop where the masons are cutting stone to repair the castle walls dynamited by the Germans in 1917, and we were on our way.

Our route took us through the huge forest of Saint Gobain, along a straight forest road with very few cars and an awful lot of cheerful birds. Soon we were getting too warm in our jackets and needed to take them off.

Sadly, yesterday's storm meant the forest tracks - which would have been more direct - were like a quagmire, so sticking to the road added a bit to the distance but it was easy walking, even when we had to turn on to a route nationale. An elderly cyclist on an electric bike stopped to talk to us. He turned out to be Dutch. Were we doing the Via Francigena, like him? No, we'd never heard of it. It turns out it's a route from Rome to Canterbury - and we were on it. So far everyone has assumed we are walking to Santiago de Compostela, so that made a change. But we are definitely not walking as far as Rome.

Eventually we emerged from the forest and descended via a winding road from the plateau to the plain. Laon, our destination, appeared before us, like the Emerald City - a long way away.

We walked through a couple of villages, the first we had encountered in six hours of walking. We laid private bets on what facilities might be offered. Fiona was right: one café (permanently closed), no boulangeries.

Cessières did have an interesting First World War memorial. Every village in France has its memorial, usually dating back to the 1920s. This one was stark and modern - but there was no explanation why.

Walking across a plain towards a city on a hill can seem endless, the destination never getting any closer. Plus we had the knowledge that our day's walking would finish with a steep climb.

We weren't wrong. Google Maps – which, when our fingers aren't numb like yesterday, brilliantly makes sure we never have to search for our bed for the night - took us up a steep pedestrian path. We got to the top, turned left - and there was an even steeper and longer path. We emerged beside the city walls with views for miles across the plain. The city's cemetery flanked the path and had the best views. A plaque told us there were war graves there, but we couldn't find them among the monumental 19th century family vaults.

Our hotel tonight is a 17th century coaching inn (with interesting 1970s details). One suspects that it was probably taken over by the Germans during their occupation of the city for almost the entire First World War. It probably wouldn't have had bright pink striped wallpaper in the bedrooms then, though.

Good day, sunshine

On this day 1916: Zeppelin raid on East Coast and Scotland – nine killed, 30 injured.

Day 17: Laon to Chamouille
Miles today: 10
Total miles: 237.5

Laon is a lovely town sitting up on its hill. It survived the First World War almost intact - albeit with its population reduced by about three-quarters - though the owner of our old hotel told us as we checked out that the back of her building was destroyed in a WW2 bombardment.

If you are ever in the Laon area, take a look. It's a charming place.

We had a shortish walk today, which we felt we deserved, though these things are determined more by the existence and availability of beds than by our choice. Never mind, we didn't set the alarm and we enjoyed a leisurely breakfast on a café terrace before setting off through a medieval city gate.

Like last night, we took one of the steep paths out of town... happily, we were going down this time as this path was even steeper.

A huge billboard at a road junction was advertising the hotel where we are staying tonight. It, rather optimistically, told us we were two steps from paradise. Paradise sounds good, but we reckoned the Fitbit might have something to say about the "two steps". Back down on the plain, and after a visit to a fortunately-placed boulangerie for lunchtime supplies, we were heading south

in bright sunshine. Sunglasses and Nick's hat were retrieved from our packs.

We've been thinking recently of how much life in France has changed in recent decades, so we were surprised to pass a man on his knees at the edge of a field cutting grass with a sickle. We exchanged words, though we're not quite sure what they were as he spoke with a very thick accent. We think we heard "bon courage" - not for the first time. We'd wondered too about the plastic lilies of the valley decorating the cakes in the boulangerie, and the children selling bunches of real ones outside. Turns out it's a French tradition celebrating the beginning of May dating back to 1561, when King Charles IX started presenting them to ladies of the court.

There is also an old tradition of "bals de muguet" (lily of the valley dances), where single young people could meet without permission, the girls dressed in white and the boys with muguets in their buttonholes.

Despite Fiona's concerns about heading off down a muddy track, we enjoyed a gentle stroll (apart from the steep uphill bit) along a section of a Grande Randonnée long-distance hiking route. First through woods, then over some open downs, dotted with wild flowers.

We stopped to rest in a village and realised that the architecture has changed enormously: suddenly we were among old vine-clad houses built of limestone, just like our home further south in Périgord.

This antiquity ended abruptly at our next stop, in Monthenault, where the signboard told us that only five houses remained in the village in 1918. On this occasion, it was because of shelling by the French, attacking Germans behind their lines on the Chemin des Dames (of which, more tomorrow). We sat on a bench eating lunch beside the rebuilt church, which was described as an Art Deco masterpiece. Or you could call it a monstrosity. The reinforced concrete is not ageing well but, to be fair, the effect of the blue stained glass on the interior was impressive.

An easy walk downhill and we reached our hotel for tonight. It's a golf resort hotel beside a man-made lake, and it's a bit of a step up compared to some of our overnight stays. Good online price, though, and there don't seem to be too many guests at this time of year.

Skip this bit if you are uninterested in domestic detail, but our early arrival meant we could get some washing done. When travelling so light, it is important to get clothes drying early. Nice to have a balcony overlooking the lake - but mainly for faster drying. And then some tricky planning for the next stage of the journey. It's surprisingly time-consuming plotting a route according to where we can lay our heads, while remaining somewhere close to the Western Front.

Some long walks are now planned for next week, and maybe some busy roads, but first... a day off. We've decided to spend two nights in Reims this weekend.

Where better to be than champagne country in the admittedly unlikely event of Fulham winning automatic promotion back to the Premier League on Sunday?

The road of death

On this day 1916: Battle of Verdun – French success at Mort Homme.

Day 18: Chamouille to Pontavert
Miles today: 12
Total miles: 249.5

The Chemin des Dames - the Ladies' Way - sounds so innocent. And for many years it was.

It was created in the 18th century to make it easier for the two daughters of Louis XV ("les Dames de France") to visit their friend the Countess of Narbonne-Lara at the Chateau de Boves.

Its history since then has been much more violent.

The road runs along a ridge, commanding superb open views on a fine day. And that is why it became so notorious.

It was here that the trench warfare of 1914-18 began, as the Germans dug in along the ridge, taking the high ground as they so often did.

The British Expeditionary Force dug in on the lower ground in front of the ridge - and the two sides kept extending their lines in the race to the sea, until they reached the Channel in Belgium.

As the British forces moved north, the French took over this sector and it remained quiet until 1917 when France's gung-ho new military commander Robert Nivelle (who was half British) convinced his government that this was the place to break through the German lines and push on to victory. He must have been a persuasive talker because, in hindsight, the idea of sending troops up a steep and heavily defended hill sounds pretty crazy. And rightly so, as the attack was a disaster.

Nivelle's aim of surprising the Germans fell apart for two reasons: one was that bad weather held up his assault so the heavy and extended bombardment of 6.5 million shells was a bit of a giveaway, and two was that the Germans knew about it anyway as they had captured a French prisoner who had plans for the attack in his pocket.

What was supposed to be a decisive 24-hour breakthrough went on for days. The result was massive losses - and a mutiny among the French soldiers, who weren't so stupid that they couldn't see what was going on.

This morning's walk took us uphill from the Ailette valley, where the Germans kept their reserve troops, to join the Chemin at Cerny-en-Laonnois at the road's centre. This village was rebuilt on its present site after the old one several hundred metres away was wiped out.

Today it is home to a memorial chapel and a lantern of the dead. It also has a huge cemetery holding not only the French-born soldiers who were killed but also many of the Senegalese who were brought to France to fight and suffered terribly. One curiosity of this cemetery is the grave of British private Albert

Truton, who was shot for mutineering but who is still listed as "Mort pour la France".

An easy slightly undulating walk took us to the Caverne du Dragon (Dragon's Lair), which makes for a fascinating visit. We'd been there before, years ago, but decided to revisit - with perfect timing as the only English tour of the day was about to begin.

We were the only people on the tour and our guide was brilliant.

This cave, one of many on the ridge, was an ancient underground limestone quarry that was taken over by the Germans. It was safer than being in the trenches and had a well, but the air was foul and it must have been terrifying when bombardments above threatened to bring the roof down.

During the course of the war, the cave changed hands several times - and in 1917 it was occupied for several months by both the French and the Germans, living in darkness and silence on each side of thick defensive stone walls. Every so often the silence was destroyed by terrifying explosions and gunfire between the two sets of tenants.

As in so many other places, the ridge was totally devastated by the war, with the land being stripped back to the bare limestone. It's a wonder that anything was able to return - and that the fields ever became cultivated again.

An information board quoted the stark post-war account of Romain Darchy, who wrote: "We are in the middle of the battlefield, in these frightening surroundings which will forever be the shame of mankind. No matter how one is looking, one can't see a living thing in this desolated nature. On the right, on the left, everywhere, everywhere the earth is shattered and burst open.

"Communication trenches, so eroded it could barely be called trenches, crisscross the cursed plateau where stretches only battered and rusty barbed wire, or small wooden crosses which hid what were once brave soldiers. If one makes an effort to look hard at this immense cemetery, one may discover here and there a severed head or a leg emerging from the ground, if not a whole corpse.

"We are at the Chemin des Dames, such a painful memory. What a derision to be still using this name here today! The ridge bearing this name is nothing but a succession of excavations and craters obstructed then covered. Of the road, nothing, absolutely nothing remains."

The fields were cleared and the road repaired, but our guide told us that the iron harvest is still bringing in 30-60 tonnes of ordnance every year in this region alone.

And the Chemin's violent history didn't end - or even begin - in 1917. A short distance down the road we stopped for our lunch at the Hurtebise Farm crossroads, where there are three memorials. One recalls the battle that took place there in 1814, the last victory of Napoleon, who spent the night at the farm. Another recalls 1917, while a third commemorates fighting that took place on that spot in 1940.

Continuing along the ridge, we skirted some woods where trenches are still clearly visible in the undergrowth, stopped at a statue of Napoleon surveying the battlefield, and then wandered among the sparse ruins of Craonne. This once-prosperous village is now just a jumble of grassy bumps among the trees as, similarly to Cerny-en-Laonnois, a decision was made in the 1920s to rebuild a short distance away.

The village is celebrated in the title of a 1917 French anti-war song, the Chanson de Craonne, also known as Adieu La Vie (Goodbye to Life). The song, which later featured in Oh What A Lovely War, was sung by the mutinying troops on the Chemin des Dames and, as a result, was banned in France until 1974. One of the few visible remains of the village of Craonne is a smashed gravestone lying among the bumps, all that remains of the church where Napoleon's casualties were once taken for treatment.

This land has seen some turbulent times.

Bring on the bubbly

On this day 1917: French take Craonne and trenches on a three-mile front, 17 miles north west of Reims.

Day 19: Pontavert to Reims
Miles today: 19
Total miles: 268.5

Walking is free, and it doesn't conjure up a champagne lifestyle - but this walk doesn't come cheap. Every night we need accommodation and we always need to eat.

This point was not lost on our daughters, who are always quick to spot any action on our part that is likely to eat into their inheritance. So it's good when we can find somewhere that is self-catering, as it gives us an opportunity to economise. A trip to the supermarket rarely costs as much as eating out - even something modest like a pizza (though we have not been reduced to eating pizza, the French national dish, yet).

Tonight we are in Reims, champagne capital of the world, so our apparthotel's cooking facilities might encourage us to splash out on some fizz tomorrow.

You might think that our day began pretty frugally as we went without the hotel breakfast, but this was only because Nick did a recce last night and discovered that the village where we were staying had - wow, a first! - an "artisan boulangerie".

Any fears that this had been a mirage melted away as we bought breakfast pastries, a sandwich and a ham croissant (and a coffee for Fiona) from a charming young man, who told us he had been baking and running his shop for seven years.

Perhaps there is hope for French villages if they can find enough young artisans and entrepreneurs. Last night's hotel was a recent creation and was excellent. Its restaurant served more than 20 covers - far more people than were staying at the hotel – and it was a Thursday night. It even had a spa.

We set off south, crossing the Aisne, but were thwarted in our plan to avoid the map contours and follow the canal because someone had omitted to provide a towpath.

Instead, we headed across country, taking the hills in our stride and enjoying the pretty villages on our way. This was glorious walking in fine early summer weather, with only the village memorials as reminders of the war and no sightseeing to do.

Contours can be deceptive, we discovered. We designated a village along the way as our lunch stop, and reached it sooner than expected simply because Nick misread those contours. He had expected a steep climb to Hermonville - instead we had a rapid descent. And this was the point at which we encountered our first vineyards. We were entering champagne country and the plots of vines in front of us on the chalky hills were pinot noir and pinot meunier, the grapes that would be blended with chardonnay to produce champagne.

Our lunch stop proved to us that we were moving into more prosperous country. This is a region with shops and restaurants. We celebrated by buying a cold Orangina before the village boulangerie closed for lunch.

From now on, the villages were all about champagne. Not the grand houses, but in these villages every modest home seemed to be a champagne house. Look at the vineyards, and it's easy to spot the patchwork of plots. Each parcel of precious land is owned by a different family, and we saw many of those families tending their vines, often on their knees.

Eventually - after a long, hot walk - we arrived on the outskirts of Reims, and our final approach on a hot afternoon was eased by a stroll along the canal, now with a towpath and taking us closer to the city centre.

A middle-aged cyclist stopped us, wanting to know where we were from. He had immaculate English with little accent and joked that he was from England. He was friendly and chatty but we were tired and wanted to reach our destination.

The inevitable question: what did we think of Brexit? What can we say? Here in France we feel so at home. Who in their right minds would not want to be part of this? Our new friend was pretty clear.

"Brexit is a catastrophe for Britain."

And on the 20th day

On this day 1916: Second Battle of Ypres − Germans gain a foothold on Hill 60.

Day 20: Reims
Miles today: 6 (sightseeing)
Total miles: 274.5

Nineteen days of walking and it was time for a rest. Twenty-one consecutive nights of sleeping in different beds and it was time to wake up and remember where the bathroom is (Nick got up one night this week and stood frozen in the dark - he had no idea which way to turn).

So Reims.... a chance for a lie-in and a bit of city life. More importantly, of course, it ensures our next few nights make more sense as they involve a Sunday night (where to eat?) and - yet another - bank holiday on Tuesday.

Reims is a fine city, the champagne capital, but it has been knocked about a bit in two world wars.

The first caused massive damage but the city recovered well. The spectacular Gothic cathedral was shelled and caught fire, and it was nearly 10 years after the war that the nave was repaired. It was finally reconsecrated in 1938, thanks to donations from around the world.

It has beautiful stained glass windows that have somehow survived from the medieval period, but also modern masterpieces by Marc Chagall and others that were a gift of reconciliation from Germany. The rest of the city wasn't entirely razed so some lovely old buildings remain, but in between there are some superb art deco houses and offices. The food market is an art deco wonder, as well as a living, breathing daily market. The food is superb - and the accordionist playing outside was pretty good too.

We bought cassolette of rabbit in a Reims mustard sauce and green beans to eat in our room. We've become huge fans of apparthotels, and although they might be limited in their cooking potential, a food market like this makes eating in easy.

On a warm sunny day, Reims (pronounced Rance, not Reems) is full of life and everyone having a good time. The bars and restaurants are teeming with locals and tourists enjoying a glass of something, usually fizzy, and there is prosperity in the air making it easy to forget the dark days of the 1940s.

Many inhabitants were tortured, deported or killed by the Nazis, and a garden square has been created in the space left by the demolition of the house where the Gestapo tortured their victims. Plaques recording the horrors that befell residents of houses around the city have been collected in this little park as a reminder of what can happen when nationalism takes over from internationalism. A stone in front of the cathedral conveys a message of reconciliation, marking the occasion when French president Charles de Gaulle and German chancellor Konrad Adenauer visited the cathedral together in 1962.

Did we mention that Reims was the capital of champagne?

Obviously, we couldn't leave without drinking some, so we headed to the gloriously over the top Cafe du Palais, with its art deco stained glass, to take a flute at a table outside. Cheers!

VE-Day minus one

On this day 1917: French successfully resist all German counter-attacks on the Aisne – 29,000 prisoners taken by French.

Day 21: Reims to Courmelois
Miles today: 13
Total miles: 287.5

The people of Reims are a bit miffed with Stalin. They appear to think he stole their glory.

We started today with a visit to the Musée de la Reddition (museum of the capitulation), which commemorates one of the city's finest moments: the signing of the Nazis' unconditional surrender in 1945. We were happy because entry to museums in

Reims is free on the first Sunday of the month. Reims is not so happy - because Stalin insisted on the surrender being signed again on Soviet territory in Berlin.

The result is that everyone celebrates VE-Day on May 8 - even though the first document was signed by General Alfred Jodl in the early hours of May 7 1945.

The Supreme Headquarters of the Allied Expeditionary Force had been set up in this school in Reims, apparently in the belief that the Wehrmacht and Luftwaffe would never think of looking for it there (and most of the building is still a school today).

This morning we visited the room to which Jodl was brought, which still has all the wartime maps on the walls. The original table and chairs are also there, labelled now with the names of the American, British and Soviet officers who witnessed the signing.

On our tour of the First World War Western Front, it was something special to be in the room where the war it led to was finally brought to an end.

We walked out of the city, on a wonderfully sunny day, thinking it would be a good idea to stop at the next café we saw. Obviously, we didn't see one.

Hundreds of people were out strolling, running, cycling. Presumably none of them was interested in spending any money? What was that spoof quote attributed to George Bush about the French having no word for entrepreneur? The only open shop we saw was a boulangerie - and customers were queuing down the street. Clearly no demand.

We joined the towpath of the Canal de l'Aisne à la Marne, fringed with trees that provided some shade from the powerful sun.

There were a couple of reminders of the First World War along the way: first an old concrete bunker beside the towpath, then the huge French cemetery at Sillery. We are now well beyond the British sector, so these regions are less well-known to the British for their wartime histories, but the Marne, Champagne and the Argonne were the scenes of major battles - and huge French losses. To be honest, it was a bit of a slog in the heat, not helped when the towpath was interrupted by bridge rebuilding, requiring a detour.

Spirits were further dampened by the commentary from Birmingham, bringing bad news of Fulham's attempt to win automatic promotion back to the Premier League. Each of Birmingham's three goals - ending Fulham's 23-game unbeaten run - was greeted with a pained silence from the Fulham FC commentator.

This wasn't a long walk but the heat and the late start meant we were definitely flagging as we approached our destination. Though Nick discovered one way to speed Fiona up: we left the canal and took a track through the woods.

It was a good shortcut - and the insects buzzing around us meant that Fiona definitely found a second wind and started walking faster.

We've got some miles to cover this week, and the forecast is for more of this heatwave so an earlier start will be a good idea tomorrow.

Choices of routes are limited as we have to avoid two major military camps. That means we will also miss Suippes, where there is a First World War "interpretation centre" (guess that's what they call museums these days).

Who could resist this (from the leaflet): "Come and dare getting into the trench which will quickly locate you at the heart of a terrible attack, thanks to the many screens surrounding you, to the images shown above your head, to the shouts of soldiers going to fight and to the machine guns balls grazing your eardrums, you will not get out of this screening unscathed. Fright flicks guaranteed."

We're sorry to be missing it.

Three battles, and Attila was the Hun

On this day 1917: Daylight aeroplane raid on north east London – one killed, two wounded.

Day 22: Courmelois to Bussy-le-Château
Miles today: 19.5
Total miles: 307

We are in the Marne, halfway between the front lines of the First Battle of 1914 and the Second Battle of 1918.

Yet we walked all day with little sign of war.

We ran out of our excellent Linesman trench maps a long time ago - the maps that gave us an idea of what happened 100 years ago or more in the land we were crossing - as they covered only the British sector. With Linesman, we saw fields of wheat, barley or potatoes, yet knew that at one time the landscape had been transformed by a new kind of "civilisation".

Once trenches had scarred the land, and military engineers created a whole new world of violence. Now all we see is crops. And it's the same here. We walked all day, but apart from guessing which churches were old and which rebuilt, there was little clue to what had gone on.

We left last night's chambres d'hôtes (B&B) in Courmelois, impressed that the village still had a 12th century church. Then we discovered the nave had been rebuilt in the 20th century after being destroyed in the Great War.

We stayed last night in the home of a farming couple called Lapie and guessed that this is an old local family. It's a bit of a giveaway that the village's main street bears that name. And on

the outskirts of the village we recognised some monumental sculptures. We'd seen these huge figures, carved by chainsaw from enormous logs and then blackened, at the Caverne du Dragon on the Chemin des Dames, and in Reims. It turns out they are the work of artist Christian Lapie - cousin of last night's host.

To be honest, we hadn't been looking forward to today: a long walk, a forecast of heat, and little choice of route - two big military camps at Mourmelon and Suippes requiring that we spend a long time on a main road. In the end, it was better than expected. It WAS long and it WAS hot, but there was a breeze, and - most important - the main road wasn't as busy as feared. There were often minutes between the cars and lorries passing us, rather than the constant buffeting we had expected.

It was only later, after we had passed a major junction, that the traffic increased. We were flagging and could have done without the truckers and van drivers - a minority - who thought it was a great idea to blast their horns as they passed. We stopped to rest our legs at the camp of Attila, a Celtic fortress that was allegedly the site of a battle involving Attila the Hun in 451. Several cars pulled up while we were there, but their occupants seemed more interested in emptying bladders than in history.

We arrived eventually in Bussy-le Château, where we were greeted at the chambres d'hôtes with the most delicious and refreshing cold apple juice (yesterday it was grape juice). There are times when something as simple as pure fruit juice is better than the finest champagne.

This village provided a railhead during the First World War and a hospital for the troops. And in the churchyard are eight graves from the Second World War: the crew of a bomber that was shot down in 1943. It seems extraordinary now to read that the pilot was just 20. These days you might be nervous to get in a car driven by a 20-year-old. In those days they were piloting bombers. As we have noted before, so much conflict and death in these regions.

But tonight we enjoyed a cold local beer and our hostess cooked us a superb four-course meal. So we go to bed (to use a cliché – and what's the point of being a journalist if you can't use a cliché?) tired but happy.

The bells, the bells

On this day 1916: Anzacs in line in France.

Day 23: Bussy-le-Château to Sainte-Menehould
Miles today: 19.5
Total miles: 326.5

We set the alarm this morning, ready for another early start on a long walk. But we needn't have bothered. The church bells across the road started ringing at 7am.

Perhaps they do that every day, or maybe it was to mark the anniversary of VE-Day (Moscow time, rather than Reims time, obviously). May 8 is a public holiday in France.

We set off (and got our kicks) on route D66, aiming for neighbouring village St Rémy-sur-Bussy, where - wonder of wonders - we had been told there was a boulangerie. There was, and it was open on a holiday. But it wasn't that helpful.

"Avez-vous des sandwichs?"

"Non."

Still, we got some cold drinks that we wrapped in our quilted jackets in our rucksacks to protect from the sun, which was getting hotter earlier than we might have liked.

Today was as long a walk as yesterday, but we chose to avoid the main roads. We couldn't face any more long straight roads with no features along the way, so instead we took minor roads with hardly any traffic. Also, sadly, hardly any shade, and hardly anywhere to sit down. This was wide open big country. For lunch we half-leaned and half-lay down against a bank under a tree by the side of the road. It wasn't the ideal picnic spot but needs must. As we passed through villages we realised the architecture was changing. We suddenly noticed half-timbered houses.

It was getting hotter as the breeze dropped and our destination didn't seem to be getting much closer.

When we finally found a bench to sit on, it was totally exposed to the heat of the sun and by this time we had all but run out of water. This was when Nick remembered a tip he had read: find a cemetery. Sure enough, there was a tap in the village graveyard and the water was cold and clean.

Every walk comes to an end at some stage, and we trudged into Ste-Menehould (pronounced Sant Men-a-OOL, or just Sant Minoo) just as the pig's trotter festival was winding up.

Pig's trotters are a big deal around these parts and the fête, and drinking, had been going on all day.

We're not sure how weird we look after more than three weeks on the road, but some people just stared at us. And not in a good way. One man laughed and told us St Jacques was in the other direction.

It was a relief to reach our hotel room. Though when we wandered out later, feeling a bit fresher after a shower, we discovered a very pretty and unspoilt 18th century town.

This is where Louis XVI was recognised as he fled Versailles for Austrian-controlled Flanders. Apparently, he made the mistake of trying to buy something in a shop - with a coin that had his picture on it.

He and the rest of the royal party made a dash for it, but were apprehended in Varennes, where we are headed tomorrow.

In the Crown Prince's lair

On this day 1916: Battle of Verdun – French success north west of Thiaumont Farm.

Day 24: Ste-Menehould to Varennes-en-Argonne
Miles today: 16
Total miles: 342.5

Some days you stumble across something interesting along the way. Today we stumbled across something we had always wanted to see.

We've talked about serendipity, and about how we don't want to over-plan. We don't need a list of must-sees as we walk - partly because it would probably mean too many diversions, and too many extra miles. So today's route was planned in the hotel lobby after checking out after breakfast: through the forest and over the hill, up the valley, and then through more forest and over another hill to Varennes.

What we realised only when we were well on our way was that our route took us past the "abri du Kronprinz" - the bunker of Crown Prince Wilhelm, who commanded the German Fifth Army.

But more of that later...

We have to say we were very taken with Ste-Menehould. Unlike so many towns, it seems to have survived the First World War almost intact. Its squares and streets are lined with the same 18th century houses and public buildings that Louis XVI would have seen when he stayed the night after fleeing Paris.

It was a major medical town and supply centre between 1914 and 1918, with even the town hall converted to a hospital. So it wasn't surprising that as we walked out of town we came across a massive French war cemetery.

It is hard to convey the scale of these cemeteries. Graves are usually back to back in French war cemeteries, so every visible cross represents two graves. And unlike in the Commonwealth cemeteries, the French put unidentified bodies in mass graves, rather than giving each body an individual grave.

Gravestones are concrete crosses on a metal frame, with a small metal nameplate attached – a much cheaper arrangement than the British engraved Portland stone slabs, but perhaps the French can be forgiven as their post-war rebuilding programme was dauntingly colossal.

We've said we like serendipity, so we are always interested in unexpected discoveries along the way.

As we walked through the woods, we heard a noise behind us. It was a wild boar, followed by her three babies. The forest was fenced in, so we can only assume she associated humans with the provision of food. And probably the same humans who will later appear with shotguns and rifles as members of the local chasse (hunt).

"Watch out for your feet," we warned her, remembering the pig's trotter specialities of Ste-Menehould (last night we enjoyed pig's trotter risotto).

As we approached the next village, with its half-timbered architecture so different from the building styles of Flanders, we found a monument to three French soldiers shot at different times to set an example to others.

Out of the forest, we followed a straight road down a valley with buttercup-filled meadows on each side. We had left behind the huge cereal fields and were once again seeing cows grazing.

At Lachalade, where we stopped for lunch under a tree, we were surprised to see the ancient abbey still standing, even though the village was razed. Apparently, the abbey was saved as combatants recognised that it was being used as a hospital.

In the abbey's cemetery, just like in Bussy-le-Château, were the graves of the crew of a Stirling bomber, shot down as they flew a mission to Germany.

In this village too was a memorial to the Italian soldiers who fought and died here - volunteers who served alongside the grandsons of Garibaldi.

Further up the valley, we turned right into the forest, by the ruins of destroyed hamlet Four de Paris. Immediately, and for the first time since the Chemin des Dames, we could clearly see trenches in the woods.

It seems extraordinary that these relics have survived for 100 years or more.

It's funny too how nobody ever describes pine woods as cheerful or inviting. Here the pine trees reached perhaps 100ft towards the sky, with little sign of any active forestry. After the First World War, many areas of France were designated "Zones Rouges" - red zones, or areas that were no longer capable of supporting life, because of poisoned soil or buried armaments.

Many areas have since been recovered, but some, such as the hills around Verdun, were simply planted with pines as it was believed no other form of life could survive. These hills felt like that.

Signs warned that the woods were private property and everyone should keep out "pour votre securité" - for your safety. Whether that was because of buried explosives or because of land-owners with shotguns was not made clear. The pine woods certainly lived up to their image as gloomy and uninviting.

As we climbed a seemingly endless hill - though nothing that any resident of the Pennines would describe as steep - we passed a demarcation stone. These were placed along the Western Front after the war to mark the extent of enemy incursion. This was only the second we have seen on our walk.

The original plan was to place one of these stones every kilometre along the Western Front. In the event, a list of 240 locations was drawn up – 28 in Belgium and 212 in France.

Only 118 of the stones – topped by a sculpted helmet – were put in place before enthusiasm waned in 1927. And, of those, 24 were destroyed in the Second World War.

And so to the Crown Prince's bunker... 750 metres from the road, but well worth the extra walk. Wilhelm, sometimes known as the Butcher of Verdun and a man who would later cosy up to Hitler in the hope that he would reinstate the deposed imperial family to their "rightful" position, allegedly used these well-appointed bunkers. They are now set among trees, so it is difficult to imagine how that blasted scene would once have looked, but the trenches that linked them are still there. No attempt has been made to restore the bunkers or protect them. There isn't even a proper car park.

But Fiona insists there IS a spooky feeling to the place. It's a fascinating site - but it was almost a relief to return to the main road and continue our walk down to Varennes-en-Argonne on the plain.

The Argonne was the scene of the Americans' major involvement in 1918, and we saw our first memorial to those "Dough Boys" as we walked into town. While they no doubt turned the fortunes of the Allies in the latter stages of the war, they suffered huge losses, in large part because of their inexperience and lack of training.

Passing a memorial to the capture of Louis XVI and the royal family, we crossed the river Aire - a nice link to West Yorkshire -

to our home for the night: a traditional French hotel now being run by a young couple.

The pre-dinner beers at an outside table went down well – especially the Tripel Karmeliet that was recommended by our host. Brewed from a monks' recipe dating to 1679, its alcoholic content probably means that one is enough.

So we moved on to wine over dinner, during which we got talking to a couple of Swiss friends who are touring the battlefields without their families. One was a former very senior officer in the Swiss army who retired without ever having to fight anyone – the best sort of military career. He even became commander of a military academy.

The two men were both witty, urbane and fluent in several languages; a fine example of how Europe should be. If we had all been like that 100 years ago, think how many lives might have been saved.

And if more people were like that nowadays, think how much more easily we could all get on together.

Horrors of Dead Man's Hill

On this day 1918: British eject Germans from front trench north west of Albert.

Day 25: Varennes-en-Argonne to Marre
Miles today: 16.5
Total miles: 359

It's hard to imagine a hill more appropriately named than Mort Homme - Dead Man.

Never mind that its name predated the war and probably referred to a tree struck by lightning on a then unforested hill (Mort Orme - Dead Elm). The French soldiers didn't miss the significance of its name, and neither did the Germans, who called it the same thing (Toter Mann).

It's on one edge of the Verdun battlefield and was the scene of ferocious fighting as the French and Germans battled to take control of it and its views over the whole area.

After the war it was designated a zone rouge where life was unsupportable and it was eventually covered in forest.

We approached it along a track from Esne-en-Argonne, crossing a field which was once the French front line. Instead of arriving up the road by car, like most visitors, we walked up a forest path.

It was immediately obvious that the ground under the trees was churned up like a lunar landscape: trenches, shell holes, craters. It didn't take much imagination to strip away those trees and see the devastation that was left in 1918. At the top of the hill, a signposted walk created by young French and German people in the last

couple of years took us down trenches and between the trees, thinned out now to make the turbulence in the landscape unmissable.

Informative noticeboards gave us first-hand accounts from both French and German soldiers of the horrors that took place on this hill. Particularly terrifying were the stories of life underground in the German tunnels that were constantly targeted by the French - and the struggle involved in digging out comrades who had been buried by shellfire.

Walking through the woods, with the birds singing, it took an effort to picture these scenes, but it wasn't impossible. Though it has to be said that the two noisy small boys running around with the couple following us down the paths didn't do much to help us connect spiritually with the past - why do boys always have to act like boys..?

We walked down to look at the hill's main monument, with its stark skeletal statue. Ils n'ont pas passé, reads the inscription - they did not pass. That was when we noticed the handful of visitors driving right up to the monument, as if walking was beyond them. At the risk of sounding smug, there is something virtuous about walking, and we have begun to feel this quite strongly.

As cars race past us on the roads, or when we see drivers display impatience that they are having to brake for a couple of seconds to get round us, we have become increasingly aware of the pleasure of travelling slowly. We see cars, lorries, speeding motorbikes, high-speed trains and think: what's the rush?

Today was a much easier day for walking. It was cloudy with a cool breeze. We thought it might rain, but that held off and the day ended with sunshine, albeit a lot cooler than of late.

Early on, we passed the hill of Vauquois, now so innocent-looking, but once the scene of unimaginable horror. Both the French and the Germans drove tunnels into the hill and set off 519 mines under it. It's hard to imagine how insecure life must feel when you are in constant fear of being blown up.

We stopped to eat the remains of yesterday's sandwich in Avocourt, like so many villages totally destroyed by the war and since rebuilt. It has the distinction of breaking one of the post-war iron rules: religious symbols were banned from war memorials, but one of the few survivors of the pre-war village was its fountain cross - so Avocourt was allowed to incorporate that cross into the memorial.

A "comfort break" took us up a track where we picked up a piece of rusty shell - although huge amounts of iron remain buried in the fields, it is sometimes remarkable how little physical evidence there is above ground. But there were a couple of reminders of how this country has been scarred by more than one war: the first was a roadside memorial to three men of the

resistance executed in 1944. The other, when we stopped for the second instalment of our lunch in Esne-en-Argonne, was a notice informing us that future president Francois Mitterrand was shot in the shoulder in the village while fighting for France in 1940.

It was Mitterrand who held hands with Helmut Kohl in Verdun in 1984 as a symbol of reconciliation.

As the final notice at Mort Homme said: "You are probably going to leave Dead Man's Hill now and return home. What you must never forget is that 100 years ago countless young French and German soldiers were denied the opportunity to do just that. Tens of thousands of them lost their young lives here on this part of the battlefield, never again to return home to their families. We must never forget the fate that befell them. Their memory is an exhortation to cherish the friendship between our two countries and continue the pursuit of European unity."

There's nothing to add to that.

Here's our fort for today

On this day 1915: Second Battle of Ypres – Germans bombard Ypres-Menin road.

Day 26: Marre to Verdun
Miles today: 15
Total miles: 374

There's an old joke that goes: "How many Frenchmen does it take to defend Paris? Nobody knows... it's never been tried."

Probably best never to try telling that joke in Verdun. The battle of Verdun in 1916 resulted in the deaths of 163,000 Frenchmen. Another 216,000 were injured. The Germans, who lost 143,000 of their own, never broke through to Paris. Having said that, the French generals did make a major defensive error early on that probably cost many thousands of lives. Douaumont was the largest of a ring of forts that were built in the late 19th century to defend Verdun. But when the French commanders saw how rapidly the Germans overran the forts in Belgium in 1914, they reckoned Douaumont wasn't up to the job and left it very lightly manned with veterans. When a German raiding party tested out the fort's defences, they were amazed to find no resistance. The soldiers refused to go in as they suspected a French trick, so a Sergeant Kunze went in alone - and took the fort single-handed. Needless to say, an officer who turned up later, Oberleutnant von Brandis, took the credit and it wasn't until the 1930s that poor Kunze's heroism was finally recognised in Germany.

This was supposed to be an easy walk into Verdun for us today, but Fiona suggested at breakfast at the quirky and Hobbity Village Gaulois hotel – with its proprietor who insisted on kissing all the female guests' hands - that we ought to go first to Douaumont. It seemed daft to come to Verdun for the first time and not go to the most important sector of the battlefield, so we set off towards it. Almost immediately, a tower appeared on the horizon - the lantern of the huge ossuary on the hill. We walked towards it, through two villages and over the River Meuse. A track across a field led to the forest edge, just like yesterday, and we headed uphill.

It seems that walking every day does strengthen the leg muscles. We realised we were able to walk two miles uphill without stopping for a breather. A friend said recently that we must be "superfit". Maybe not SUPERfit, but there's no doubt that walking is great exercise.

It seems few people approach the summit by the walking route, and halfway up we found the ruins of an old prewar concrete emplacement that had been the scene of fierce fighting. As had a partly-shattered command post a little further up. They are among the trees now, but these scenes were once exposed to ferocious fire. At the top of the hill is the ossuary, like a kind of art deco concrete version of the Palm House in Kew Gardens - but with thousands of crosses on the lawns in front. The ossuary holds the remains of 130,000 unidentified soldiers (and 80,000 more are still lost somewhere in the surrounding forests).

In front of the ossuary lie 16,142 identified French soldiers in the largest French military cemetery of the First World War. It was inaugurated in 1923 by Verdun veteran André Maginot, who would later lend his name to the French defensive line intended,

unsuccessfully, to deter future German invasions.

Onwards, up the hill past more ruined bunkers and the "London trench", a communication trench built of concrete slabs − some of which remain - to the fort itself. A huge amount of work has gone on here recently to create a new car park and disabled access and at the moment it looks a bit of a mess. One can only hope that time will soften it - as it has the battlefields and the grassy surface of the blasted fort.

Entrance to the interior is a bargain at four euros. The moment you walk through the door, you feel the chill - literally and metaphorically. Everything is damp − mainly because the concrete

walls and roof were cracked by incessant bombardments. This is not somewhere you would choose to spend a lot of time.

Considering the smashed-up exterior of the fort, the interior is remarkably intact, even down to the impressive machinery for raising and lowering the heavy turret guns. Many men died here, but the worst incident was self-inflicted. German soldiers used flamethrower fuel to heat some coffee, and exploded a store of shells, sending a firestorm through the corridors. The bodies of 679 German soldiers killed by the explosion were bricked up behind a wall - still a war grave to this day.

It was good to feel the warmth of the day as we emerged from the damp chill, but we still had a bit of a walk into town. We passed a rough bit of ground which Nick had to walk across to read the small notice. The notice revealed that this was land that was left in its original unlevelled condition after the war. Rather belatedly, given the position of the sign, it asked visitors to avoid walking on the ground.

Fortunately, the rest of the walk was all downhill and we found a track that bypassed the busy road. There weren't many other walkers as we descended between the trees, wondering about those 80,000 men whose bodies were never retrieved.

So tonight we are in Verdun, a town that resonates with the French in the same way that the Somme does with the British. We thought this was one place where we would have no trouble finding accommodation. It turns out there isn't as much accommodation here as we thought and most of it was booked up, so we have ended up in our most expensive hotel of the trip - three times as costly as the place we stayed on Wednesday.

We expected a classy, traditional sort of place but, disappointingly, it has been infected with the modern French passion for lime green and grey. You can't get away from it, however much you pay. And we won't be having the breakfast: at 16 euros, it's more expensive than a five-course lunch with wine at our favourite local restaurant in the Dordogne.

So what did we learn today? Obviously, that it's best not to use flamethrower fuel for cooking - especially when there are high explosives nearby.

But also - and it might sound like a cliché - we have been reminded of the futility of war. Why is it a cliché? Because it's true. And because the deaths of all those hundreds of thousands of young men ultimately achieved nothing. Military experts might argue with us, perhaps, but what did the deaths at Verdun do to advance the cause of civilisation?

A trench – but not that kind

Day 27: Verdun to St Maurice-sous-les-Côtes
Miles today: 21
Total miles: 395

It was a long day, but it was a tale of two roads - and the first was the one that led out of Verdun.

We were both surprised by Verdun: we somehow expected a mean little rebuilt town, burdened by the weight of history. Instead - and admittedly we only scratched the surface - we found an attractive town on the banks of the River Meuse, with some fine monuments and many of its old buildings intact.

Our hotel last night was converted from the 19th century officers' mess on the river bank and we crossed the bridge and passed under the 14th century Porte Chaussée to find our breakfast. A handily-placed boulangerie in the pedestrianised street provided bread and pastries for eating at a table outside, plus a couple of sandwiches for later. Even with lunch included, we saved a fortune on the hotel breakfast.

As we left town we admired some proper "old France" buildings and streets, as well as the old fortifications. Given the fate of so many towns and cities near the front line, how could Verdun - with its constant bombardments - have fared so well?

Sadly, the outskirts haven't. The road out of town took us past all the grim shed-shops that are to be found in the suburbs of all French towns these days. For the first third of today's walk, we had to stick with the main road out of Verdun, which wasn't that busy but, equally, wasn't much fun either – not least because of a massive valley we had to descend and then climb again on the other side. At least the weather was kind to us.

The road was marked with columns telling us that we were following the Voie de la Liberté (Liberty Road) - the route taken by Allied forces through France after D-Day in 1944.

We were already feeling weary as we finally reached our turn-off, taking us over the Autoroute de l'Est and into the forest, where we were relieved to find a picnic table under the trees.

From this point we were walking a trench - but not a First World War trench. La Tranchée de Calonne (Calonne's trench) is a long straight road through the forest created by one of Louis XVI's ministers who had bought a château in the area.

That's not to say we had got away from the Great War. This area saw heavy fighting from the very start of the war as part of the St Mihiel Salient, and shell craters were easily spotted from the road, along with the occasional memorial.

But the forest has literary connections too: Alain-Fournier, author of modern French classic Le Grand Meaulnes (sometimes translated as The Wanderer or The Lost Domain) died here in the first month of the war, bringing a premature end to a promising career as a writer.

His masterpiece was published in 1913 – one year later he was dead, aged just 27. His body lay undiscovered until the remains of more than 20 soldiers were excavated in a clearing in the early 1990s.

He and his comrades have since been reburied in a war cemetery, but the scene of his discovery has been protected with a glass canopy, stones to mark where each of the bodies was found, a sculpture and a French flag.

Along the same path are remains of old trenches, and two underground German bunkers that it is still possible to enter. On the German side of the forest, Ernst Junger, author of Storm Of Steel, fought here too. He survived both wars and died in 1998.

This was a long, long road and walking it became quite hypnotic. In about 20 kilometres we passed no sign of human habitation - just trees on both sides - which is astonishing to anyone who lives in the tightly-populated UK.

At one crossroads, we read some wartime experiences of the area on a noticeboard and were able to compare an old picture with the scene today at that exact spot. Yet again we were struck by the contrast between the peace of today and the violent turmoil that once ravaged this land.

We didn't regret the diversion off the road to see the relics, but the kilometres continued to rack up as the day wore on. The forest was a beautiful and calm place, but it offered nothing more in the way of rest. A couple of times we had to perch uncomfortably on felled logs, swatting the inevitable insects, just to take the weight off our feet for a few minutes.

We looked forward to a left turn that would remove us from this endless road, but even that left us with some walking to do before we reached the hairpin bends that led us down the steep slope to our destination.

We finally arrived in St Maurice-sous-les-Côtes, at the foot of the forested plateau, after 7pm, as the church bell reminded us. Like so many other French villages, this one seemed to have seen better days. There were some fine houses, but not in great condition.

It was eerily quiet as we walked down the street – but Fiona told Nick to move to the side of the road. "You look like Clint Eastwood walking into town in a Western," she said.

It has been a tiring day. Luckily, tomorrow should be a lot shorter (especially as the weather forecast is not good). Fiona has been struggling with her hip, and after more than 100 miles this week already we probably need a rest.

A plum posting

On this day 1915: Second Battle of Ypres — very severe German bombardment.

Day 28: St Maurice-sous-les-Côtes to Heurdicourt-sous-les-Côtes
Miles today: 7
Total miles: 402

Today the waterproofs came out again - and the temperature plummeted. Luckily, this coincided with a day when we had been forced to plan a short walk to the next hotel.

Accommodation, as we might have mentioned, is few and far between in these parts. So occasionally, like today, we have to book places that aren't so far between to avoid desperately long walks.

Times are tough for the catering business in France. Our hotel last night used to have the village bar, but it closed seven years ago. The current owners took over five years ago and tried reopening the bar but nobody came, so now it is used only as a breakfast room for hotel guests.

St Maurice-sous-les-Côtes is an odd little village that probably never recovered from the First World War when the Germans took it over and deported all the working-age men for forced labour. They kept the women, children and elderly there as human shields against French bombardments.

It was eventually liberated by the Americans in 1918, but less than a quarter of a century later it was occupied again. Perhaps it is not surprising that a notice in the nearby German war cemetery revealed that that it had been damaged by vandals. We're now in wine country, even though many vineyards were replaced by orchards after the First World War. Mirabelle plums are everywhere: in the sauce on last night's veal chop, in our breakfast jam - and even in a beer we were offered before dinner.

At one of the villages along the way we stopped to read about an American B-17 bomber that crashed in a nearby field during the Second World War. You can't get away from war, one way or another, round here.

But, amazingly, we were able to get out of the rain for a few minutes. In the village of Vigneulles-lès-Hattonchâtel we found a bar that was open. The customers, enjoying a pre-Sunday lunch glass of something, and the owner welcomed us in as we dripped on the floor.

Several were drinking the local white wine from green-stemmed hock glasses, but we settled for coffee and hot chocolate. It was good to get out of the chilly wind. And as the customers drifted off to their lunches, we took to the road again, knowing we didn't have too far to walk.

We were grateful to reach tonight's hotel in good time and have a few hours to relax. We were so early that the lunch service was still in mid-flow as we reached reception but the lovely staff didn't seem to notice our drowned-rats-with-backpacks appearance.

We were happy to pay a supplement for a room with a bath, which was filled more than once with lots of comforting hot water. During the afternoon we spent a couple of hours trying to find accommodation for the two nights after next Wednesday. If anything scuppers our plans to reach the Swiss border, it will be the lack of beds. We'll keep trying. Today we passed the 400-mile mark, so we don't want to give up now.

We mentioned earlier the trials of the modern French hospitality industry, but here's a funny thing. This village appears to have no more life in it than last night's – yet this hotel seems to have no shortage of customers. The rooms are pleasant though nothing special, but a lot of money has been invested in the restaurant and it has clearly paid off.

Three large dining rooms were pretty much full when we arrived, and even tonight - a quiet Sunday evening – there were other customers enjoying a very good dinner. Maybe it really is true: you build it, they will come.

We've seen this elsewhere in France, where so-so restaurants struggle to stay alive while others that really make the effort have no trouble bringing in the punters.

Dinner got off to a great start when we were offered the house cocktail. It was superb... not surprisingly, perhaps, it featured mirabelles.

Walking in border country

On this day 1917: King George tours industrial centres in the North. Engineers and London buses on strike – weavers in North threaten strike.

Day 29: Heurdicourt-sous-les-Côtes to Pont à Mousson
Miles today: 20
Total miles: 422

What's it like to find yourself living in the same place but suddenly living in a different country?

In the UK we might find ourselves out of the EU next year, but it's unlikely we will ever wake up to find ourselves living in France or Germany. Which is what has happened to people living in this area in the past.

This morning we walked out of the Meuse and into Meurthe and Moselle - and parts of this region have switched backwards and forwards between France and Germany.

The weather forecast for today wasn't good and we set off in drizzle in our waterproofs. By mid-morning, though, we had taken off our rain trousers and at lunchtime we shed the jackets. The rain had stopped and the day was warming up. But the cloud was low and it was a strangely peaceful day in this part of la France Profonde.

As we walked along country lanes, we seemed to have left the war behind. When we reached a junction with a straight main road, we took a majority decision to turn on to it, rather than follow our planned route. Google Maps agreed - it didn't even offer the route we had planned as an alternative. Immediately we spotted a wartime blockhouse, and down the road was a destroyed village with a novelty: a stone that recalled events in BOTH world wars on one column.

A path led away from the road and through the trees to the church of the ruined village. It was unmarked, but a deep and clearly visible trench ran alongside the track. Perhaps these

trenches are so commonplace as to have become invisible to local people.

Another track took us off the main road and led us down to our destination. As we looked across the field to the busy road, we realised we were probably walking on the original road that would have taken troops into the town, long before the fast modern road was built.

At the start of this walk we wondered what sort of road surfaces would have been familiar to our grandfathers as they went to war. We've since realised that this sort of rough track is probably exactly what they marched on in those days before everything disappeared under tarmac. This was another long wearying day of walking, and we can expect more this week as beds for the night have been hard to find. You would struggle to describe Pont à Mousson as pretty - and tonight's hotel can fairly be described as basic - but the town has its points.

For a start, on a Monday night, we found a restaurant that was not only open, but was packed out. Again, it seems that people will turn up if you provide what they want.

The town also has plenty of boulangeries for lunch - and a small supermarket that should supply tomorrow night's dinner. There's no hot food available at our next stop so we will be relying on a picnic.

Nominally about Nomeny

On this day 1916: Sir Roger Casement charged with high treason for his efforts to gain German military aid for the Easter Rising in Ireland.

Day 30: Pont à Mousson to Alaincourt-la-Côte
Miles today: 16
Total miles: 438

Today was a lot about Nomeny. It wasn't our final destination, but it might as well have been. All morning (after a night disturbed by tremendous thunderstorms - and possibly the aftermath of Fulham's playoff win) we walked along another of those endless straight roads that was probably built to take Napoleon's troops to Russia - or more likely back again. Those roads stretch out forever into the distance, with the uphill bits seemingly outnumbering the downhill sections.

And with plenty of lorries passing us. Nomeny had been nominated by us as our lunch stop, but at times it seemed we would never eat again. Round a bend....still no sign of Nomeny. Then another... Eventually we walked into this small town on the River Saille. We had our sandwiches and were ready to look for a bench.

But what do you know? There was a hotel/restaurant at the side of the road. It was open. There were people eating. Admittedly, it was late for lunch by French standards - 1.30pm - but we sat down at a table on the terrace. And so it was that we ate our first cooked lunch of the trip. OK, so it was only omelette and chips but as we'd been expecting sandwiches for lunch and a picnic for dinner, we were pretty pleased. Nick even had a beer.

This was exactly the sort of place we feared was totally lost in France: a Hotel du Commerce, with its bar, terrace, dining room - and table football.

Nomeny has two war memorials, one on each side of the river: the first is for the soldiers and the other for the civilians. As in so many places, the local people here suffered badly at the hands of the Germans. The town was occupied by the Germans on August 20 1914 and the governor of Metz, General von Oven, ordered its destruction as a reprisal for an alleged attack on Bavarian troops by civilian snipers. The town was plundered and burned down, with around 55 women, children and elderly people slaughtered.

After Nomeny, the walk became easier, passing through villages such as Mailly-sur-Saille, where the château was occupied by Germans in both wars, and was bombed by the Americans in 1944. The village is still guarded by a crumbling blockhouse, now facing modern suburban homes. Outside the village cemetery, French fighter pilot Maxime de Ginestet is buried under the war memorial. His plane came down just behind the château.

We mentioned our lunch, and here's the funny thing. We are using up a lot of energy (Fiona's Fitbit tells her she is regularly burning 3,000 calories or more) so we ought to be ravenous. Yet Fiona couldn't even finish her omelette. Sometimes we are offered three courses in the evening and we try to eat it all, but left to our own devices we will eat just the one dish if we go to a restaurant. Maybe there will be less of us when we get home.

No danger of three courses tonight. Our lodging is in what we suspect was the servant's quarters of the priest's house in Alaincourt-la-Côte – Allenhofen to the Germans. It is a simple cottage attached to the old presbytery, where our hosts now live, but they have done an extraordinary job in converting the upper floor to a spectacular bedroom and shower room. Mrs Doyle wouldn't recognise it.

Sadly, our hostess cooks meals for guests only at weekends, so we sat downstairs and ate our simple picnic. In Pont à Mousson this morning, after crossing the bridge over the Moselle, we had stopped at a riverside bench and decanted a bottle of claret into a plastic water bottle to make it easier to carry.

Wine, cheese, pâté and bread. What more do you need? Oh yes, we had chocolate too.

How many shades of grey?

On this day 1915: Zeppelin raid on Calais.

Day 31: Alaincourt-la-Côte to Château Salins
Miles today: 12.5
Total miles: 450.5

We've seen a lot of changes in the architecture in our month on the road, from the grim brick postwar reconstruction in the north to the almost alpine style of the Argonne. Recently the churches have taken on an Anglo-Saxon appearance, with spires that look almost English.

All along our route, new-builds are going up with scant regard for traditional local architectural styles. One thing they all have in common is the use of multi shades of grey.

Grey doors, grey shutters, grey roofs, grey garages, grey windows. Even grey stripes on the external walls. It is as though the entire housebuilding industry has been handed over to a naval dockyard. The only relief is provided by the ubiquitous purple and lime green giant plant pots.

Before we had even left last night's village we had noted probably half a dozen new homes, and all of them had been designed using just a palette of grey. It was possibly quite chic to begin with. Now it just looks depressing.

The direct route to Château Salins was along a main road so we tried to avoid it as much as possible. We began on a disused railway line which had us wondering what life was like in those pre-car days when every village had a station, whether here or in Britain. We imagined strolling down the lane, or possibly taking a horse and cart, to the disused station that is now a private home and waiting for the steam train to arrive and take us to the next town.

In that next town, Delme, we were surprised to find a synagogue and an old Jewish cemetery. The synagogue was last used for services in 1978 and is now an arts centre, but it turns out that Lorraine once had a thriving Jewish community.

Nearly a fifth of the Delme population was Jewish.

When the area returned to German control during the Second World War, the synagogue was dynamited by the Nazis.

It was defiantly rebuilt in the 1950s, but the population of Jewish families was by then much reduced and, as numbers continued to dwindle, the synagogue eventually had too few members to be viable.

We turned off the main road again for a quiet detour... well, quietish, because as we walked along a back road along a ridge, three open-top and British-registered Morgans sped past.

We had just had time to Google prices for secondhand Morgans when another two came by, one of them tooting and giving us a wave.

Life on the open road.

Sadly, we had to rejoin the main Strasbourg to Metz road to approach Château Salins and we were reminded of how joyless most motor travel is these days. But at least it was all downhill from there.

Escape to the chateau

On this day 1916: Daylight Saving Bill passed — from now on clocks will be put forward for summer.

Day 32: Château Salins to Tarquimpol
Miles today: 17
Total miles: 467.5

Last night we stayed in a modern house that was built and furnished like a château. Tonight we are staying in a real château.

And the great thing in both has been the eating: it's like being a guest at a dinner party.

Our lovely hostess last night cooked and served for the two of us, another English couple and three young Frenchmen who were in the area to work.

We got on so well with the English couple that one of the French guys asked if we were travelling together and how long we had known each other.

No, was the answer to the first question. Two hours, the answer to the second. That's the great thing about the French chambres d'hôtes system: everyone eats at the same table.

This evening we shared a table with five other delightful guests, mostly speaking French, and the château's charming owner. It seemed that all the other guests had pretty high-powered jobs, at least one of them to do with the EU. This being France, the conversation was pretty highbrow (including the inevitable comments about Brexit), though it seems most people were here for the local bird-watching. We felt a bit grubby but were given the thrones of honour in the grand salon at aperitif time as soon as everyone heard how far we had walked.

Tonight, as on every occasion, the food and drink was excellent - proper home cooking rather than fancy restaurant cuisine. If you're visiting France, do think of trying a chambres d'hôtes instead of a chain hotel. It's the closest you'll get to being invited to a house party.

When we said goodbye to our hostess and our new friends this morning, it was cool enough for Fiona to wear a jacket. But a steep hill, a cruel start to the day, meant the jacket didn't last long. By noon it had become a glorious summer's day.

We passed through a sombre village called Moyenvic. Our first thought was it had been destroyed in the First World War but the damage actually happened in 1944, when it was at the centre of a major battle involving American and German troops.

A quick Google search brought up a detailed account of the battle. It sounded grim.

When you walk through these places you can feel a shadow over them, said Fiona.

That's not just because of the 1950s rebuilding. Or because of the controversial and vast cubic church that was built after the remains of the original medieval building were razed.

As we left the village, Nick scrambled down a bank to find a quiet moment behind a tree - and spotted curly barbed wire stakes being used to make a fence. First World War or Second? Did the Germans still use them in the Second World War? Maybe there's an expert out there who could tell us.

We stopped for lunch in an extraordinary place. We had walked off the main road and turned a bend - and gasped. This was just a little village, but the old gateway was enormous. Marsal (the clue is in the name - this area became wealthy on the salt trade as it sits on the world's biggest rock salt seam) was fortified by celebrated military defence builder Sébastien Le Prestre de Vauban in the

17ᵗʰ century after Louis XIV seized Lorraine. The village retains its shape, and the medieval names of all its streets.

Like most places round here, the village once had a German name – Salzmar – but all its streets now bear their old French names. There's no May 8 1945 Street here, or Charles de Gaulle Square, as you often find elsewhere.

Little evidence remains in the region of these German occupation names, unless you look carefully... later we passed a disused railway station and spotted the fading station sign. The French name had peeled off, leaving the German one faintly visible.

Oddly, Alsace and Lorraine have different laws to the rest of France due to the German occupation. Cannily, as our host at the château pointed out tonight, they managed to keep everything they liked about German law and re-adopted all the best bits of French law. They're not stupid.

Walk. Just walk...

On this day 1917: US congress passes Army Bill – 50,000 troops to be mustered in September.

Day 33: Tarquimpol to Blamont
Miles today: 18.5
Total miles: 486

Throughout the history of mankind, humans have put one foot in front of the other and walked. If they didn't have a horse, donkey, mule or ass, that's how people got around.

They didn't wear specialist walking shoes and they didn't have digital navigation devices. They just walked.

It was only the arrival of the railways, followed by the inventions of the bicycle and the motor car, that changed all that. And allowed us to forget the simplicity of walking.

Some people have said they envy what we are doing and wished they could do it too. Well, it's not difficult. Obviously, you need a certain level of fitness (though walking makes you stronger as you go along), you need the time and you need the money to do exactly what we are doing, but there's no need to go to such "extremes".

Just walk.

It is physically and mentally healing. We are feeling freer, happier and fitter than we have probably ever done.

Fiona, who has been told to call her orthopaedic surgeon whenever she wants to get a replacement hip, is feeling less in need of that operation now than she has for a long, long time. We were both a bit worried at the weekend as she was starting to walk at an alarming angle, leaning towards the kerb as we walked on the left side of the road.

She wondered if this was to do with balance issues connected to sinus/ear problems but, after an internet search on Sunday, she reckoned this was a side-effect of the prescribed anti-inflammatories she has been taking.

Naproxen has helped ease her hip pain, but apparently it also causes vertigo – especially, and most relevantly, in women over 60 who have been taking a full dose for a while. So she reduced the dosage by half - one pill at bedtime - and immediately she was walking straighter.

Neither of us knows how long it takes to reduce the side-effects of this sort of medication but both of us know the power of the mind-body connection, and this was a perfect demonstration of that.

Today we set off with sandwiches in our packs. Last night's host at the château was the first person we have come across to think of offering us sandwiches, and he made them himself as a gift.

It was a glorious day, so we ignored the warning of a somewhat unlikely risk of snow that we passed on a road sign and made the best of a largely minor-road walk.

There was a mile or two on our old friend the Metz-Strasbourg road (though walking in the opposite direction to before) but we turned off on to a lane with almost no traffic.

Totally unexpectedly, we walked into the scene of one of the major social/industrial/agricultural experiments of the 20th century.

First, we came across Hellocourt farm - an unfeasibly huge structure for a country farm. There had to be more to it.

And there was. In the period of German occupation between the Franco-Prussian war and the end of the First World War, this farm was acquired by a German engineer, who rebuilt it at the turn of the 20th century and applied modern scientific agricultural principles to increase returns.

The German was expelled in 1919 and the farm was taken over in the 1930s by the Bata shoe company.

Bata was a hugely successful Czech company run on paternalistic lines and, just down the road from the farm, it built a whole village around a new factory: Bataville.

It was in the middle of nowhere, yet it employed and housed thousands.

It was only towards the end of the 20th century that Bata finally pulled out, apparently because – funnily enough - the French workers and unions refused to go along with the old paternalistic rules.

The factory finally closed in the first decade of this century.

All the factory buildings are still there, as are the workers' homes, the church and the communal buildings. People still live there - but the village has a ghostly atmosphere. It felt odd to walk through it.

Tonight we are in Blamont, and we had high hopes. Sadly, the town seems as depressed as many we have walked through. We struggled for the first time to find our room for the night – and when we did, it seemed we weren't expected. As we stood wilting on the doorstep, a window opened and the face of a mystified woman appeared.

I had emailed a confirmation of our booking several days ago, but the woman said her husband hadn't received it. It was a rather worrying moment as we were exhausted and it seemed unlikely that we would find any other rooms around here.

Luckily, one of her three rooms was free – the other two had been booked this morning. A sigh of relief but then we discovered that our restaurant booking for tonight wasn't much use – because it was in a totally different Blamont. Major communications failure today. The good news: this town has one restaurant. We found it and even though today is a Friday, there was no problem at all getting a table. Clearly not much cash available to be spent round here.

But we are now ready to launch an assault on the mountains of the Vosges. We're not quite sure what to expect - but we have already modified our itinerary to shorten Sunday's walk. Let's see how it goes.

Climb every mountain

On this day 1918: Bombing of British military hospitals at Etaples, outside war zone, by German airmen – 300 casualties.

Day 34: Blamont to Pierre Percée
Miles today: 12.5
Total miles: 498.5

The Vosges mountains appeared on the horizon a couple of days ago. Now we are among them, in a village beside a lake.

We'd been forced to deviate from our original intended route for a couple of days by the need to find beds for the night, but today we were right back in the thick of it. We stopped at a village called Montreux to read the local history panel and discovered that the Germans forced the local men, women and children to work on the roads in the early days of the First World War - before giving them half an hour's notice to leave their homes in early 1915. As we left the village we spotted the blockhouse and the remains of other concrete emplacements. Then, further on, the pine woods were a giveaway. We knew what they signified, and trenches and shell craters were soon clearly visible on both sides. We were back on the front line.

We walked into Badonviller, on the edge of the Vosges, where a crippled Second World War tank still commemorated the battle for the town in November 1944. Sadly, the town doesn't seem to have moved on much since then.

We had already started climbing, as our legs informed us, but the road out of Badonviller took us up into the forest - more pine trees – and into what must have been a particularly inhospitable zone for soldiers.

Today it was beautiful in the sunshine and the birds were singing but it must have been grim fighting here, or even not fighting here, in the winter.

Our hostess tonight told us that many of the young French soldiers who fought here were Corsican, and their parents sent them chestnuts in the belief that they would help to keep them fit and healthy. Many of those soldiers were killed and their chestnuts were lost - until they began to grow after the war.

The chestnut trees in the area were tested and, sure enough, they were Corsican.

She also told us that two RAF parachutists landed in the village during the Second World War and were taken in by the then owner of the house where we are spending tonight.

They were hidden from the occupying Germans until they were fit enough to take an escape route - only to be shot before they could reach safety.

She told us that the son of one of the two airmen came to stay here and was able to retrace the steps of his father. Oddly, our host last night told us over breakfast that a British couple were staying in his gite. She was the daughter of an airman who died, aged just 21, when his Lancaster crashed nearby on the way back from Germany in 1944.

So on our way out of town this morning we visited the local civilian cemetery, where he and his seven fellow crewmen had been buried by the local Red Cross. On each grave there was a poppy wreath laid by the daughter of that young man.

This morning we were commenting on how odd it is that the

French have so many superb long-distance footpaths, yet we have seen almost no one walking.

Immediately, we spotted a man and woman walking at pace on to our road at a junction. We exchanged greetings and they sped off ahead of us up the hill.

After our lunch break, we were walking uphill in the forest when they overtook us again, now accompanied by another woman. "We are walking the First World War front line to Switzerland," the man announced. "So are we!" we said. It turns out that they started a week after us and are planning to finish in 36 days. At that pace they will no doubt do it - but they had another advantage over us.

They are supported by someone in a car and their itinerary is planned in advance for the whole trip.

This means they don't have to carry anything more than a daypack and, more significantly, unlike us their route is not dictated by the availability of hotels.

They walk a direct route and are collected at the end of the day to be taken to the nearest hotel. Next morning they are returned to their starting point.

The extra woman turned out to be man's wife, who had started walking with them today only after lunch and was therefore keen to walk at a tremendous pace.

We would have taken a picture of them - but they had rushed on before we could ask.

Barbarity knows no nationality

On this day 1916: British regain mine crater on Vimy Ridge.

Day 35: Pierre Percée to St Dié-des-Vosges
Miles today: 17
Total miles: 515.5

This is a difficult thing to write. We set off on this walk determined that this wasn't only about commemorating one "side" over another.

The First World War wasn't just about British sacrifice. It wasn't just about French loss. It was about the waste on all sides, whether victors or losers. One thing has impressed us all the way through: the ability of the French people to forgive.

In Reims we stood on the spot where a French president and a German chancellor agreed to put their troubled past behind them. Everywhere we go, the flag of the EU flies among those of the individual nations. And yet...

Tonight we are in St Dié-des-Vosges, a town that has a dreary appearance despite its position on the River Meurthe and the beauty of the circling forested hills. Why is it dreary? Because in November 1944 the town's occupiers set everything ablaze as they retreated.

Here's another question: why did they deface the town's memorial to the dead of 1914-18? Whatever the answer, when the town was reconstructed in the late 1940s and 1950s (though not by Le Corbusier, who had a radical plan for its renaissance), it was decided to leave the desecrated war memorial as a reminder of the perpetrators' barbarism. Another memorial we passed informed

 us that 970 residents of the town were deported to Germany from that spot on November 8 1944. All over northern France we have seen and read evidence of that "barbarism".

But of course it is not just about one nationality. War IS barbaric - and, as we know, it's always the victors who write the history. No nation comes away from a war with a clean conscience. War brutalises.

So there it is. And today began with few reminders of that brutality as we walked around the lake of Pierre Percée to the sound of birdsong.

Yesterday's sunshine had disappeared and rain threatened all day, but never really came. We left the lakeside road and headed for a town where we turned into a major valley. The walk gradually became less idyllic as we shared that valley with a main road and some pretty undistinguished settlements.

Our hearts sank as we saw a yellow "Route barrée" (road closed) sign ahead, but it turned out to be a vide grenier - a kind of car boot sale that everyone loves in France. In this case it stretched out along a village's long main street. Perhaps there will be some tables set out for a makeshift café, Nick said, thinking of the sales we go to in the Dordogne.

Dream on, said Fiona.

But there were - and we dropped our packs and bought an Orangina and a local beer. The Orangina (whose lack of availability in the closed shops along our walk has made it a prized treat) was the usual colour. The beer was green.

We love a vide grenier as much as the next Frenchman and - inevitably, as the last thing we wanted to do was buy extra stuff to carry - this one looked tempting. But we walked on, eventually reaching the outskirts of St Dié, where we were astonished to find a food shop open on a Sunday afternoon. It sold halal meat, among other things, and was doing a roaring trade with all manner of French customers, who - as is well known - never want to go shopping on a Sunday.

In town tonight we shivered outside a pizza restaurant - yes, after five weeks we finally went to one - while the staff were rushed off their feet. It was probably the only restaurant open in St Dié on a Sunday night and it was rammed.

But, as everyone knows, the French never want to go out to eat on a Sunday night.

Two seasons in one hill

On this day 1917: US division to start at once for France under General Pershing.

Day 36: St Dié-des-Vosges to Ste Marie-aux-Mines
Miles today: 15
Total miles: 530.5

A magnificent day's walking in the Vosges mountains - marred only slightly by the weather. Well, marred quite a lot actually.

Weirdly, we started the day worrying about sun screen. Hats and sunglasses went on early, and our water supplies began to run low pretty soon too (we carry two plastic half-litre bottles each that we top up from the tap every morning).

At lunchtime, as we began a slow ascent, we saw people laying tables in the shade in their gardens and Fiona wondered how often the weather was this glorious round here.

The architecture had become more and more alpine and the flowery meadows were very Sound of Music. As we laboured uphill in the sunshine, graffiti on the road urged us, in French, to "Go faster, bastards" - though that might have been aimed at racing cyclists rather than us.

We sat on a bench and, just as we finished our sandwiches, felt the first drop of rain. From then on, as we climbed higher and higher, the rain jackets went on... and off... and on... until Fiona finally decided to ditch hers. It felt better to put up with a little rain than to sweat like mountain goats in a sauna in our jackets. The rain become a bit heavier, then torrential and thunder started rolling around the mountains. We sheltered for a bit, then convinced ourselves it was easing off and set off uphill again.

We were fooling ourselves. We trudged uphill getting wetter and wetter - Fiona had her rain jacket on again by now, but it seemed too late to bother with the trousers. Water was gushing down the road and swilling around inside our "waterproof" shoes.

We reached the top - the Col de Ste Marie, at 772 metres above sea level. This was the scene of ferocious fighting in the First World War: now it is the border between Lorraine and Alsace, but then it was the frontier between post-1871 France and Germany.

By the side of the road were two military graves: one from 1916 and one from 1940. A sign indicated a 14-18 military cemetery up a track but we were too drenched to visit it - or to admire the view.

We started downhill, convinced that the rain must stop soon. There was blue sky ahead of us, blue sky behind us - but the storm remained above us. Any hope we had had of arriving at the bottom of the hill steaming in the sunshine had faded.

A car pulled up and the driver kindly offered to turn around and give us a lift to town. We thanked him profusely - but refused. We haven't been in a car for more than a month and, wet as we were, we couldn't get in one now.

He said the town was a long way, which was kind of true, but it was all steeply downhill. We descended from that 772 metres to around 380 metres in the town, hurrying past signs of wartime defences of the mountain pass that was now well behind us.

We were glad to reach our hotel, where our landlady gazed at us in sympathetic horror as we pushed the door open and sloshed our way into her bar.

She rapidly led us to a room with a bath, and then pointed Nick in the direction of the dryers at the local launderette. It was the first time he had been in a launderette for some years – but the dryers did their work and we have some wearable clothes again. Our trousers had been absolutely sodden.

Ste Marie-aux-Mines gets its name from the silver mining that once made the town rich. That was a long time ago. Tomorrow morning we might get a chance to explore a bit, but our first impression is of a place that has seen better times.

We are now very much in mountain country - and German mountain country at that. We ate in the hotel restaurant tonight and the food was hearty - potatoes, cheese, pork - and beer seemed the appropriate accompaniment.

When our landlady explained the short blackboard menu, she spoke German to us, forgetting that we were English. "C'est mieux en français," Nick said - it's better in French - which seemed to cause great hilarity at the next table. But even Fiona knew what kartoffel meant.

Stormy Monday… and Tuesday

On this day 1915: German air raid on Paris.

Day 37: Ste Marie-aux-Mines to Fréland
Miles today: 15
Total miles: 545.5

If yesterday was a day of two halves, today was a day of four halves.

Technology has been a wonderful thing on this walk, but today it let us down on several fronts.

For a start, Google Maps led us to believe this would be a shortish walk, albeit hilly. Maybe Google knows of a secret zipwire over the mountains, but we were soon disabused of this idea when we saw a signpost as we left town this morning. A town that was supposed to be just a staging post was further away than we had believed our destination to be.

Then the weather: it was bright and sunny this morning as we headed uphill out of town and we had hoped to reach our room for the night before the forecast storm. That didn't happen.

And, finally, an online map led us round in a huge circle as we searched for that overnight stop, meaning we walked several kilometres too far and descended an unnecessary 200 metres in elevation - and of course we had to climb that same height up a very steep road to get back to it.

It had all started so well, with a leisurely breakfast as the sun shone outside. We even invested three euros to allow ourselves the luxury of watching our walking shoes bang around in a dryer at the launderette for 30 minutes. That's how confident we were of arriving at tonight's destination before the next storm. And Ste Marie-aux-Mines turned out to be quite a fine town after all, even though its best times are undoubtedly behind it.

As we rapidly climbed the road out of town, we commented on how alarmingly some motorcyclists had passed us at speed in yesterday's storm. Almost immediately, we passed a sign warning of "too many accidents", asking bikers to slow down. This sort of coincidence has happened so many times during our walk.

We were impressed by our climbing strength as we rapidly reached 855 metres above sea level. The Upper Calder Valley holds no fears for us now. The views were spectacular and we felt good.

Then we felt rain.

This time we didn't mess around. Immediately the waterproofs went on - and quite right too.

The rain quickly turned heavy. Then heavier. Then, just as we thought the rain might be easing, the hail started. As we dashed for cover - such as it was - Fiona's hand was cut by a hailstone.

The "cover" was pretty pointless - we were probably getting just as wet under a tree as if we had carried on walking. So, as the monsoon-style rain continued, we decided we might as well keep walking.

Fiona reckoned it was the worst day of her life. But, even before the rain finally stopped, she had rapidly reviewed her 40 years-plus of married life and decided that probably wasn't even remotely true.

The rain did stop - so that was the first two halves. And the sun came out, making the third. We managed a short lunch stop for a sandwich - yesterday's - and walked on, our waterproofs drying out.

We sat for a few minutes on a well-placed bench admiring the view over the valley where we are staying tonight, and everything felt good again. In sunshine, the scenery around here really is sensational. This is a curious little corner of France. It got its name from Freiland (Free Land) because the original charcoal-burners who settled here and made their livings from the surrounding forests didn't pay any taxes. And it is in the middle of the Pays Welche – from an old Germanic word meaning foreigner. Hence our own Welsh people and language in the UK.

Fréland is home to the Maison du Pays Welche, or Welsh museum, though we'll have to save that one for another time.

We headed down into the village where we had booked a room, guided down some very steep paths by our phone maps. No sign of the establishment so, as Fiona rested on a bench with a friendly cat, Nick went to ask in the mairie.

The mayor's secretary checked her computer, then pulled a pained but sympathetic expression and printed out a map. Our room was right back up the hill. Well, we say hill, but really it's a mountain.

So that's where we are, after dragging ourselves back up. And it was worth it – we have a huge room at the top of an old house, and our young hosts have been brilliant. No chance of going out for a beer, so they brought us one.

No chance of going down to a restaurant either, even though they offered us one of their cars (Get in a car? Not a chance). So we've eaten a modest picnic bought from the poorly-stocked village shop and life feels pretty good again.

Whoever said this walk was going to be easy? And anyway, you can have too much of eating in restaurants.

The hills are alive

Day 38: Fréland to Munster
Miles today: 18
Total miles: 563.5

The hills were alive with the sound of cow bells, birdsong... and gunfire.

The French are famously keen on hunting and we've heard gunfire close to so many former battlefields we have passed. Today we heard it in the area of one of the bloodiest but most forgotten battles of the First World War.

The Battle of the Linge took place on the summit of a mountain in the Vosges in 1915. It caused the deaths of 17,000 men on both sides - men who had lived in one of the most inhospitable postings on the Western Front.

We knew we had to cross the Linge on our walk to Munster today but when our generous host of last night offered to give us a lift down the hill into the village, we turned him down. Even though we were retracing the steps of last night - and it took us the best part of an hour to get down there - we thought it would be cheating.

Fiona had been suffering with her hip for the last couple of nights so she was struggling to get going. We stopped for a coffee in the next valley and pushed on to Orbey - a smallish town that seemed to go on forever and was on a busy main road.

In the town we spotted a plaque on the wall of a house. It informed us that from December 9 1944, during the liberation of

---

Orbey, a French lieutenant, 15 legionnaires and two tanks were surrounded by Germans for a week in that house. They eventually decided to "faire Camerone" and, as a result, the building had since been renamed Camerone Farm.

Doing "Camerone" was a new one on us, but an appeal on Facebook quickly revealed that this referred to an incident in Camerone, Mexico, in 1863 when 65 men of the Foreign Legion held off 2,000 Mexicans for a day but ended up dying. Ever since, "faire Camerone" has meant to fight to the last man.

The traffic didn't bode well for the rest of the day's walking, but we turned off that road and headed upwards, leaving the cars and trucks behind. We had decided to stay on roads in the Vosges, for safety's sake mainly, but the road up to the Linge snaked round so many hills that it was going to add a lot of kilometres.

So, trusting our map, we took a minor road up the hill, which turned into a track, which turned into a narrow footpath between bushes that brushed against us on both sides, that led up to a forest track. It was steep, but it was direct. One of the brilliant things about GPS mapping is that you always know exactly where you are.

Even when we were climbing a track that wasn't shown on the official French map, the little red circle on the tablet showed us where we were heading. And where we were heading was for the German war cemetery at the summit.

The cemetery's noticeboard carries a message from Jean-Claude Juncker: "Those who question Europe or despair about Europe should visit military cemeteries. They show what a disunited Europe, the confrontation of the individual peoples with 'don't want to join' or 'can't join' attitudes must lead to."

Amen to that.

A short distance away is the site of the Linge battlefield, extraordinarily well preserved. The small museum is excellent, but it's the superbly built German trench system that impresses - and the proximity to the French trenches. In one village that we passed last week, we read an account of a French former soldier who claimed he had been in a trench just 10 metres away from a German trench – close enough to throw stones at each other. We put that down to exaggeration.

But here, on the Linge, a noticeboard informed us that one French forward position was less than a metre away from a German fortification. THAT is close.

After the appalling battle of 1915, when the Germans were

determined to prevent the French retaking Alsace cities such as Colmar, the two sides dug in and there were no more major battles. But they spent those remaining years in shouting (almost whispering) distance of each other.

And the Germans constructed some pretty formidable defences. Walls were solidly built of local stone and cement, and defences were topped with concrete observation points made behind the lines and brought forward to be fixed in position.

Inside one such post we could read the original German graffiti scratched in the cement while it was still wet – more than 100 years ago. Huge crosses among the trenches — white for French, black for German - mark the spots where bodies were excavated in the 1960s and 70s. Signs warn of dangerous ground, where buried unexploded bombs could still pose a risk, and the rusty rolls of barbed wire are still there.

Sadly, the first heavy rain of the day began just as we emerged from the museum to wander around the trenches, so we weren't inclined to linger, but this spot would be worth a much longer visit.

And anyway, it was a long descent from the 1,000-metre heights of the Linge to Munster, where we are staying tonight, so we needed to get moving.

The man who sold us tickets in the museum laughed when we said we couldn't hang around as we had to get down to Munster. Oh, he said, it's all downhill – you can be there in two minutes!

Not quite. The downpour stopped as we set off from the Linge and although it started raining again as we descended, we weren't bothered. This was NORMAL rain, rather than the tropical storm-style rain of the last two days. By the time we reached the valley it was calm and sunny again and our clothes were dry.

This side of the mountain feels totally different. It's very German... so German that little attempt has been made to Frenchify any of the place names, as happened elsewhere after 1919.

Alsace is an odd area - officially French, but culturally German. Our friend Steve, who moved from the UK to the state of Victoria in Australia, once told us he laughed every time the TV talked about a "Victorian man". He said he always pictured someone in a stovepipe hat and a frock coat. We feel much the same when we read that restaurants are serving Alsatian specialities. These days people always seem to talk about German shepherds, but when we were young they were always Alsatians.

Which brings us to the joke of the expedition - one that made Fiona laugh, and still does. You need to have something like this to laugh at again when you are struggling at any point. And it seems appropriate in a country where our approach brings dogs running and barking to every fence.

It concerns two dogs that went into a bar.

Dog 1: I heard a great joke today.

Dog 2: OK, then, let's hear it.

Dog 1: Knock kn...

Dog 2 goes f****** mental

Keeping on keeping on

On this day 1916: Sir Edward Grey speaks in House of Commons on peace terms.

Day 39: Munster to Guebwiller
Miles today: 19
Total miles: 582.5

They might not be the Alps, but the Vosges mountains have been challenging. It's fair to say the last four days or so have taken it out of us.

We didn't know what to expect before arriving in the region - and we had to plan our overnight stays in advance to make sure we were always moving in the right direction and weren't going to get stuck up some blind valley.

The result has been some longer days of walking than we might have preferred. Yesterday that meant 18 miles, and then another 19 today. Not too bad on the flat, but the Vosges definitely aren't flat.

We were heading south today, but the first few miles were sideways to get us to a gap in the mountains. By mid-morning we were doing some serious uphill walking.

OK, so it was on a road, though fortunately a road with little traffic. And we were heading for the Col Firstplan, which isn't as high as the passes of the last two days. But it was relentless. We continued uphill for nearly two hours, each bend revealing yet another incline to be conquered before the next one. And the next one... We finally reached the top at lunchtime, knowing there were still plenty of miles to go. Cumulative weariness was setting in after several days of this. A picnic table gave us a few minutes' rest as we ate our sandwich and consulted the map. Was there an alternative to continuing on the long windy road?

Fortunately, there was – we found a forest track that took us downhill much more quickly than the road, so that saved us a lot of walking. And it gave us a chance to look up the latest on the growing wolf population in the Vosges.

We didn't see wolves, though we did hear barking in the forest. A dog... or something else? We did see some deer, startled by a pair of humans appearing on foot. At least the weather was kind. The only light shower - not enough to make us put on waterproofs - came as we walked past the Maison de Fromage (Cheese House) early on. The clouds cleared, and as we descended the sun came out.

The meadows round here are wonderful: full of wild flowers. Fiona is happy living out her Heidi fantasies. But it was a long way (and we had to climb again to another col). By the time we dragged ourselves into Guebwiller - a town we had never even heard of until last week - we were exhausted. Luckily our hotel tonight has a decent restaurant.

Don't suppose we need to book for dinner, we said to the hotel receptionist. Oh yes, you must, the hotel owner is playing his guitar tonight. Really? Yes, really... the huge restaurant was completely booked out to eat and to hear the boss and his band play. Actually, the food and the band were pretty good.

One nice touch: a glass of crémant d'Alsace for every hotel guest. The carafe of local dry muscat (we could see the vineyards from our table) went down well too. So well that we had to order another one.

Blue is the colour

On this day 1916: Military Service Act becomes law – congratulatory message from the king.

Day 40: Guebwiller to Cernay
Miles today: 10
Total miles: 592.5

There were cornflowers at the edge of the field as we walked today and they reminded us of the man with the collecting tin.

He shook his tin at us as we came out of a shop so we put something in and he handed us a piece of paper. He was collecting for the "Bleuets".

Bleuets are cornflowers but it was also the name given to the young Frenchmen who signed up at the start of the Great War and went into action in 1915. Cornflower blue was the colour of the uniform they wore. A poem written in 1916 by Alphonse Bourgoin finishes:

En avant, partez joyeux:
Partez, amis, au revoir!
Salut à vous, les petits "bleuets",
Petits bleuets, vous notre espoir!

(Go, and leave with joy;
Leave, friends, goodbye!
Hail to you, the little cornflowers,
Little cornflowers, you are our hope!)

In 1925 two nurses at the national home for war invalids created a workshop where wounded veterans could make paper cornflowers. Rather like our poppies.

And, just like the poppies, the cornflower tradition continues to this day.

Today was an easier day for us - and we needed it. We both woke up at about 3.30am, Nick with a pain in his calf and Fiona with uncomfortable toes. So he took one of Fiona's anti-inflammatories, then renewed her Compeed. That's the sort of thing WE get up to at night.

We took our time getting up, as we didn't have too far to go today, then breakfasted at a boulangerie in town. It was market day in Guebwiller and that felt odd: the town has a German vibe, but the market was very French.

We're now very much in a wine area, and Fiona cleverly spotted a cycling/walking route that took us off the road. Almost immediately, among the pinot and gewurztraminer vines, we saw a concrete bunker from 1917 that was built by German troops for resupplying.

Like at the Linge, the battle had been fought not down here on the plain but at the top of the nearby mountain - Hartmannswillerkopf - for domination of the land around. Sadly, today we had no energy to climb to the top, at 956 metres, so we'll have to save that one for another time. But we did walk through the village that gave the mountain its name - Hartmannswiller - and were reminded by the war memorial of one of the curiosities of this area. You won't find the words "Morts pour la France", as you do in other regions.

That's because this was German territory from 1871 to 1918, so the young men who died were wearing German uniforms.

It was a hot sunny day (everything seems to be extreme when it comes to weather for this walk) and we had to follow tracks between and around shadeless fields. At least the mountains were now off to our right and we were walking level terrain for a change, but the heat added to our sluggishness.

As we entered Cernay we saw the French war cemetery, with many slabs with curved tops in among the crosses. The shape of those tombstones reminded us once again of how indebted the French are to the men of the former colonies in Africa who came to Europe to fight and die.

They never had a chance to make paper cornflowers.

Price of the 'criminal madness'

On this day 1917: Hospital ship Dover Castle torpedoed twice in Mediterranean and sunk — six lost.

Day 41: Cernay to Carspach
Miles today: 17.5
Total miles: 610

We sat down to eat our lunchtime sandwich on a hard stone bench (they obviously didn't want to encourage loitering) outside an old chapel and in front of a rather anonymous space: the Place des Malgré-Nous.

The Malgré-Nous (Despite Us — or Against Our Will) were the men of the Alsace and Moselle who were forced to join the

Wehrmacht or Waffen SS in the Second World War and fight for Germany, whether they wanted to or not.

Most of the 130,000 were sent to fight on the Eastern Front, presumably to discourage desertion.

But some did desert to fight for the Resistance, or fled to Switzerland, though this often led to their families being deported to labour or concentration camps. And, of course, when the war ended, those men were treated with suspicion, as if they had volunteered to fight for Germany. Some of the Waffen SS troops who took part in the horrific massacre at Oradour-sur-Glane in the Limousin on June 10 1944 were Alsatian.

In 1953, 14 of them were found guilty of taking part in the massacre – but a week later, after an outcry from Alsace, the French government passed an amnesty law for the Malgré-Nous, and those former SS men were released very soon afterwards.

This time it was the people of Limousin who were outraged. But a plaque in the Alsace town of Kaysersberg says: "Alsace is the region of France that paid the heaviest price for the criminal madness of Nazism."

Today's walk, longer than yesterday's, was tough again. Partly because of the heavy heat that made walking hard going, but also because - to be honest - it was pretty dull.

We walked through villages that were clearly just dormitory suburbs for Mulhouse, just up the main road and close to the German border.

It was a Saturday, so people were out washing their cars, pressure-washing their patios or clipping their lawns. And the countryside between the villages wasn't much more interesting.

True, there were some fine examples of the traditional local half-timbered Germanic architecture, but the rest could have been anywhere in modern France.

Still, by this afternoon the Vosges mountains were well behind us and there were signs ahead of what must surely be Switzerland. The end is nigh.

Tonight we are in Carspach, close to Altkirch, and very much on the old front line. Apparently there is a deep shelter built by German troops nearby, and we passed a large blockhouse on the way into the village. Though actually we are not in Carspach, as we discovered on our arrival in the town. After checking Google Maps, Nick was horrified to discover that the hotel is actually slightly outside the town, which meant a weary trudge at the end of a tiring day again. At least it wasn't up a mountain – but it was a few minutes away from a junction we had passed a good half an hour earlier.

And Nick had to break that unwelcome news to Fiona.

He reckons that Fiona has three gears for walking: fast, when he can hardly keep up with her; medium, when we walk at the same speed; and very slow, when he is physically incapable of walking slowly enough to remain alongside her.

This evening she was definitely in slow gear.

Never mind. The hotel is excellent, the restaurant superb – and the wifi was up to the task of streaming Fulham's Championship playoff final victory at Wembley (promoted!) so all is good tonight.

Both sides now

On this day 1918: Third Battle of the Aisne begins – new German thrust for Paris.

Day 42: Carspach to Mooslargue
Miles today: 11.5
Total miles: 621.5

Last night we slept behind the French front line. Tonight we are right on the German front line.

Yesterday's hotel was totally destroyed during the First World War and it wasn't rebuilt and reopened until 1961. As we walked back down to the village this morning, we recrossed the former No Man's Land.

Tonight we are staying in a modern apartment hotel near Mooslargue, which was occupied by the Germans. Just across the valley – and what is now a rather swish golf club patronised largely, it seems, by Swiss members – is Pfetterhouse, which was held by the French. This line ran all the way from the Belgian coast to here – and not much further. A short distance away from where we are tonight is Kilometre Zero, the point where the Western Front ran up against neutral Switzerland and came to an end.

So tomorrow morning, all being well, we shall reach the end of our walk: one thousand kilometres from where we started in Nieuwpoort six weeks before.

Today's walk wasn't too taxing, which is just as well as the Vosges left little in the tank. It was hot and humid under a heavy sky, but that eased as we walked, and the scenery was more interesting than yesterday. We left Carspach along a former railway line that is now a cycle track, then passed through several villages, stopping for rests whenever we saw a bench.

We were reminded yet again of the territorial crossover between the First and Second World Wars when we stopped at a memorial to a French tank commander who died liberating one of the villages on today's route on November 20 1944. One plaque read: "A la mémoire de Isidore Ygon. Conducteur du Char Ouessant du 2eme Cuirassiers. Mort héröiquement pour la liberation de Hirsingue." (To the memory of Isidore Ygon, driver of the tank Ouessant of the 2nd armoured cavalry. Dead heroically for the liberation of Hirsingue)

Below, another plaque says, more simply: "Merci Ygon. Tu as sauvé la vie. Rominger – tank Ouessant" (Thank you, Ygon. You saved lives.... a message from a comrade).

As you pass through such villages today – the type that we tabloid journalists inevitably refer to as "sleepy" – it is impossible to imagine the violent scenes that once took place there.

One thing we have been aware of as we have been walking is the call of the cuckoo. They seem to be a rare thing in Britain these days, but we have heard them everywhere we go. Though every time we have heard one, we have joked that it is "our" cuckoo, the same bird following us and watching over us on our journey. After all, they do all sound exactly the same.

We arrived in good time at tonight's hotel, only to find that reception doesn't open until 5pm. With time to kill, we wandered down to the golf course next door. It felt like another world.

Golfers in tailored shorts stepped out of their Mercedes, into their golf buggies – who would want to WALK anywhere? – and then into the smart clubhouse where we rather lowered the tone. As we sat under a sun umbrella on the terrace and reflected on the past six weeks, we felt we had earned our beers – the most expensive of the trip, inevitably.

And so tonight, having handwashed our smelly T-shirts possibly for the last time, we are on the verge of achieving something we have thought about for so many years.

We are almost within a par 5 distance of Switzerland.

The end of the Line

Day 43: Mooslargue to Kilometre Zero
Miles today: 7
Total miles: 628.5

All good things come to an end - and that sometimes applies to the bad things too. The Western Front might have seemed endless when the two sides dug in - rather like the war itself - but it wasn't.

We began this walk at the northern end of the line, where it couldn't go any further because it reached the sea.

Today - passing the 1,000-kilometre mark - we reached the southern end, and that couldn't go any further because the neutral Swiss made sure it didn't. It's hard to imagine these days, especially when you consider Germany's disregard for neutral Belgium, but everyone respected the Swiss border.

And the Swiss made sure of it, sitting at the end of the front line like some sort of tennis umpire ensuring fair play.

In recent years a path has been cleared through the forest to "Kilometre Zero", as the end of the line is known, and some unobtrusive (ie almost invisible) markers have been fixed to tree trunks.

Concrete remains among the trees are explained, such as the German command post that was disguised with three young pine trees - one of which still grows through its roof.

Nearby, a machine gun post that defended the road bridge is still there, with its connecting trench and the shelter for its gunners. Down a forest track, the site of the end of the line has been overgrown in the past with trees, but some have now been hacked back to reveal the most southerly German wartime structures.

A concrete bunker is cordoned off with a danger sign.

Then, a few yards on, the path crosses a wooden bridge, built by Swiss soldiers in 2012, over the tiny River Largue. The other end of the bridge is marked with a Swiss flag.

We really have reached the end of the line - and we are reminded of that by the modern Swiss customs sign. Our phones ping and welcome us to Switzerland, which is not, like France, free of roaming charges. Not only the end of the line, but we have left the EU. Prophetic...

A little further on is the notorious border stone 111. This stone was regarded as the point where hostilities officially ceased. It was observed by Swiss troops in a bunker built of wood. Not concrete, because it wasn't expecting to be bombarded, though there was always the danger of a stray bullet.

And again, Swiss troops have been busy, creating a faithful reproduction of the long-lost original.

Behind the bunker is an old farmhouse, Largin Farm, which not only survived the First World War, but later became a gathering point for the men of Alsace who fled over the border from occupied France into Switzerland in 1942 and 1943 to escape compulsory service in the German armed forces.

Reaching the end of our journey - six weeks to the hour since we got off the tram at the Belgian coast - should have been a moment of elation. But when you are in such a place and you know what went on, and you see the bunkers and trenches, it is as though the ghosts of those combatants are still there too.

It is not like they are at peace. Fiona, all along, has found such places oppressive. She feels the presence of so much suffering. One thing that has struck us in recent weeks is that although the war inflicted huge wounds on the British psyche, it was actually France that was fighting for its territory. British soldiers died on patches of land that might now be forever England, but for the French this was their home they were defending.

Walking back down the French side of the front line, we joined the old trackbed of a railway that continued running until 1970. We passed the ruins of a bridge which during the First World War sheltered a railway carriage used as a French command post. The bridge survived intact - until the Germans finally got it in 1944,

Further on, a wooden sign tempted us into the woods, where we found Villa

Agathe. Not most people's idea of a villa, but this was the name given by troops to their most southerly concrete structure.

Nick ventured down the steps inside, but even a torch failed to make it any more welcoming. The fact that it has survived for 100 years means it must have been a safe refuge for French soldiers, but today - like all such bunkers we have visited - it is less than inviting. We have been fascinated to discover how much remains, a century on, of the structures that formed the front line. But that's not really why we were doing this walk.

In November we celebrate the centenary of the Armistice. Although we now know, with hindsight, that the Armistice, and the treaty that followed, was only storing up trouble for the future, it brought peace for a time.

The Great War - la Grande Guerre - became known later as the First World War when it turned out that the war to end all wars didn't. In the words of Eric Bogle's Green Fields Of France, "it's all happened again... and again, and again, and again and again". When we began walking, there was talk of a Third World War, which is, of course, unconscionable. We all know where that would lead... and it would probably be the end of the line for us all.

So... where does that leave us right now? In the first week of our walk, two people asked us what we would do when we reached Switzerland. We laughed. We hadn't thought that far ahead. Now we have had to. We couldn't get to a clearing in a wood and come to a standstill. So we retraced our steps.

Our vague romantic thought had been that we would travel home by train, but a quick check of prices a few days ago revealed that the train would cost nearly five times as much as flying. How times have changed.

But first we had to get away from Mooslargue. We could have walked, of course, but instead we booked a cab. It felt odd being in a car for the first time in more than six weeks. Cars go so fast! In a matter of minutes we had raced back over a lot of the distance we had covered so much more slowly yesterday. At that speed it is definitely harder to take anything in. No doubt we shall quickly get used to speeding around in a car, but for now it is an uncomfortable experience. We have learnt to enjoy taking things slowly.

Tonight we are in Basel/Bâle, a city that turns out to be on the Rhine (we never knew that... the only thing Nick did know about the city is that its football team was once knocked out of the Europa League by Fulham) and it is the meeting point of Switzerland, France and Germany. It is wonderfully international and totally delightful.

It's a bit of a shock to the system after all these days on the road. But that shock is being eased tonight by a glass or two of something sparking.

So the epic walk ended as it began - with a selfie. Again, no one else was around to record our presence, so we did it ourselves.

We had done it, ourselves.

What have we learnt?

Forty-three days, one thousand kilometres, 45 different beds in 46 nights... and what did we learn?

Actually, we learnt a lot: about history, about people and about ourselves. Often, we would notice something we had never seen or heard of before, do a quick search on our phones and end up educating each other via the teachings of Professor Wikipedia as we walked along.

So here, randomly and in no particular order, are some of the things we either learnt or were reminded of:

:: Perhaps not so randomly, the first thing is that this war wasn't about the British. Obviously, it involved millions of British people and touched most families in the UK, but the Western Front was really about the Belgians and the French. It was on their land.

:: Wherever you are walking on mainland Europe - and in whatever direction - everyone assumes you are heading for Santiago de Compostela.

:: Most of our lives are led too fast and we need to slow down. This particularly applies to drivers, mostly truckers and Mercedes owners, who were infuriated if we slowed their journeys by one second by daring to share a road with them.

:: The French have such low expectations of British people's language abilities that even mediocre spoken French is regarded as some kind of miraculous achievement.

:: On the subject of language, some highly educated Swiss people speak a form of German that doesn't even have a written version. Just think about that for a moment.

:: The French have an odd attitude towards pavements: they use them to park their cars on, even when there is a perfectly good road alongside, and otherwise fill them with all manner of obstacles, including lampposts, trees and large signs at head height. France is not a welcoming place to the unsighted pedestrian.

:: Walking shoes become very smelly when they get wet and are dried out. Luckily, French supermarkets are prepared for this and sell handy sprays of shoe disinfectant.

:: Walking is a great way of losing weight. Fiona's Fitbit regularly told her she had burnt more than 3,000 calories - yet our bodies decided to impose a limit on what we could eat.

:: French village life - certainly in the north east - is dying fast, or is possibly already dead: hardly any cafés, bakeries or shops survive, and boules courts are being reclaimed by nature.

:: Cold Orangina is the walker's friend. Few opportunities to buy (see above) so stock up when you can and wrap spare cans in your dirty clothes to keep them cool for later.

:: It's extraordinary what you find at the roadside. Apart from all manner of roadkill, we saw many different items discarded by passing drivers. Who throws Christmas decorations out of a car window?

:: However exhausted you feel at the end of the day, a bath/shower, 20 minutes sitting down and a beer will usually get you back on your feet.

:: French children are still brought up to be polite to strangers. Even small children would say "bonjour" as they passed us in the street.

:: A bench in the shade is a welcome sight to a walker on a hot day - and a bus shelter with a bench is even more of a blessing when it is raining. And forests are all very well, but you can walk for miles without seeing anywhere to sit.

:: French dogs used to have a bad reputation, but our trekking poles were only ever used for trekking. Dog-owners have to keep their pets fenced in nowadays... so the worst that happened was a surprise bark that made us jump.

:: It might say "waterproof" in big letters on the box that your walking shoes came in, but you can still expect to feel water swilling around inside them at some point on a long walk – even if you don't go paddling.

:: It was refreshing to discover how little STUFF we needed in six weeks. Travelling light meant carrying only one change of clothes - thereby removing any need to worry about what to wear next.

:: The First World War finished 100 years ago in November, but it left massive scars on the lands on which it was fought. Much remains to be seen, and it will continue to be visible for many years to come. And it is reckoned it will take 700 years to clear the land completely of war debris - if it ever happens.

Above all, we learned one thing: we are all capable of so much more than we give ourselves credit for. Whatever challenges we set ourselves, we might be surprised at how achievable those targets are.

We just have to step out of the ordinary.

Postscript

After we finished the walk, a bundle of old documents that once belonged to Fiona's grandfather Jack Day fell into our temporary possession. Among these documents was a sheaf of typewritten reminiscences of the First World War.

These filled in some of the details that were missing from the bare bones of Jack's military record. They explained, for example, why he never did get to receive his long-promised commission, even though he was made an acting captain in the field. We also learnt more about the footballing concussion incident – including the fact that the Prince of Wales (later to become, briefly, King Edward VIII) called in to Jack's tent to check on his post-match welfare.

Jack's typed reminiscences of the war ended with the words: "Had I learnt any lessons? Yes, many, but the chief one perhaps THAT WAR IS A WASTE… of lives and all else and anyway FUTILE, it settles nothing!"

Beneath, he added a handwritten postscript:

"A later thought: On a day in 1916 when duty caused me to cross over part of the battleground with bodies strewn by the thousands in all directions (history told us there were 60,000 of our young men killed and injured there the day before) the sky seemed to go dark and EVIL, only the Devil smiled and I vowed that if ever one got home again, one would try to get people to attack the Devil who causes war and not to attack each other!"

Jack always liked to have the last word. On this occasion, we are more than content to let him have it.

More to read

If you've enjoyed reading about our walk, you might enjoy these books too…

Back to the Front: An Accidental Historian Walks the Trenches of World War I - Stephen O'Shea (Walker 1997)

O'Shea, then a journalist based in Paris, walked the Western Front, mainly in two long sections, after being inspired by a visit to the Somme. This is an account of those walks. It is very good for its descriptions of what happened during the war in the regions he walks through. Although it is a little light on information on the actual walking, he was generously helpful with his advice to us (apart from suggesting we cycle it instead!).

The War Walk: A Journey Along The Western Front - Nigel H. Jones (Cassell 1983)

A more selective account of walking the Front, but Jones's book is an interesting companion to O'Shea's. Jones, a former PA journalist like Nick though many years earlier, is excellent on the details of battles, and - writing in the early 80s - was able to interview WW1 veterans while there were still plenty around.

The Somme Battlefields - Martin and Mary Middlebrook (Penguin 1991)

Indispensable guide to visiting the Somme battlefields, of course, but also some very useful explanations of, for example, how war cemeteries were created. The book is full of fascinating detail – so much so that it especially suits anyone touring at walking or cycling speed.

Elsie & Mairi Go To War – Diane Atkinson (Arrow Books 2009)

True story of two Edwardian women who set up a first aid post on the front line in Belgium – and became hugely famous as "the Madonnas of Pervyse".

The Battlefields of the First World War - Peter Barton (Constable, in association with the Imperial War Museum, 2008)

Expensive and weighty, this is a magisterial description of the battlefields by Barton, one of the foremost experts on the subject. The subtitle is The Unseen Panoramas of the Western Front, and the book contains dozens of panoramic views from the trenches, photographed during the war for military purposes, as well as many other pictures you probably haven't seen before. Not the sort of book you would want to carry in your pocket but great if you have a coffee table big enough.

Fields of Memory - Anne Roze (Cassell 1999)

Nick reviewed this book for the Yorkshire Post when it was published and it has remained on our bookshelves ever since. Its contemporary and modern photographs of the Western Front helped inspire us to consider this walk.

Printed in Great Britain
by Amazon